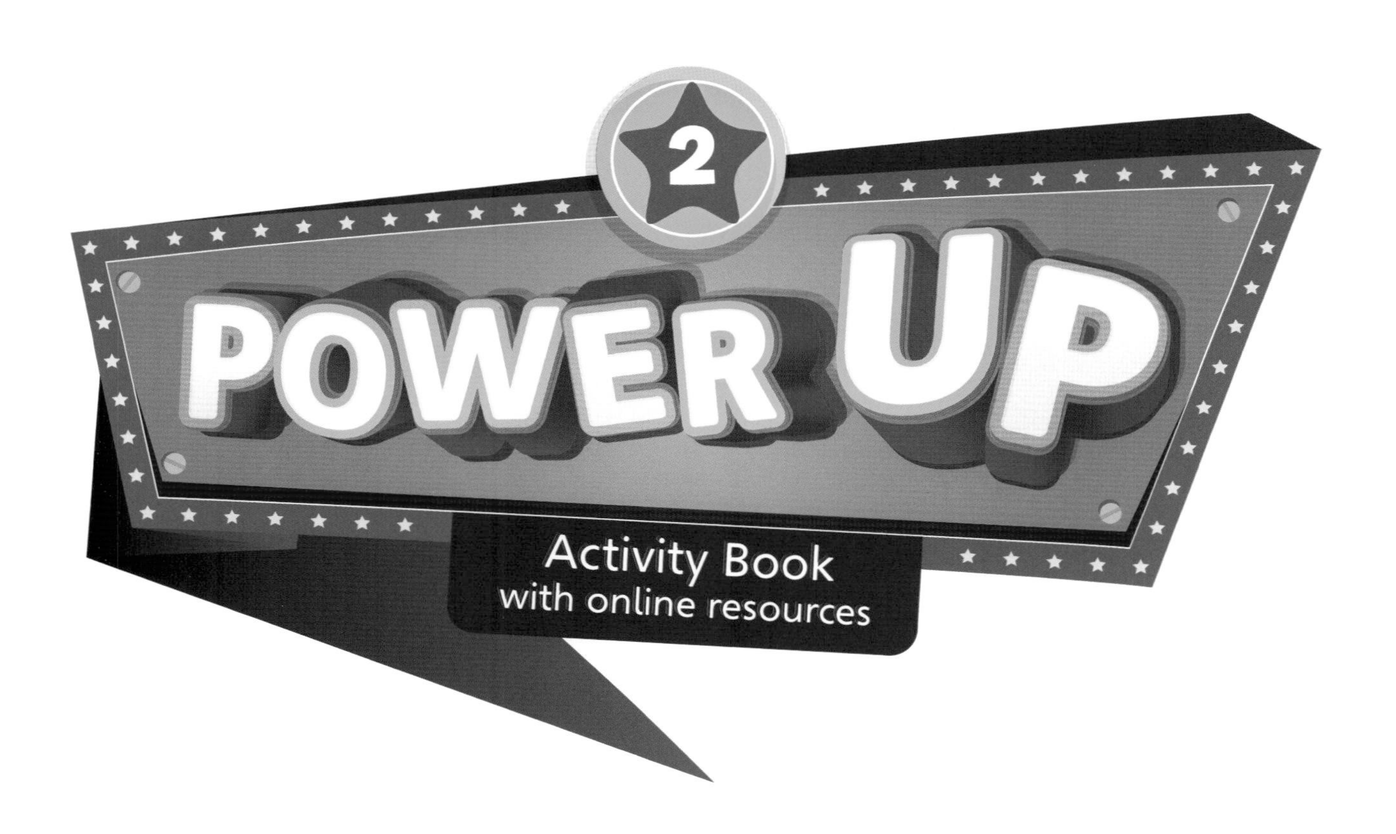

Caroline Nixon & Michael Tomlinson

Map of the book

	Vocabulary	Grammar	Cross-curricular	Literature	Assessment
Meet the family Page 4	Character names	**Personal descriptions review** *How old is she? She's five.* *He's got long hair.*			
1 A day on the farm **Mission: Make a daily routine chart** Page 6	Countryside Daily routines **Sounds and spelling:** *r*	**Present continuous review** *Are you reading a book?* *No, I'm not. I'm doing my homework.* **Present simple for routines; *o'clock*** *What time do you get up?* *I get up at seven o'clock.* *What time does school finish?* *It finishes at four o'clock.*	***Look after our planet*** Learn about how to look after our planet	***The race*** A poem Social and emotional skill: Being supportive	A1 Movers Speaking Part 1
2 My week **Mission: Plan a fun activities timetable for two friends** Page 18	Days of the week Free time activities **Sounds and spelling:** *ay*	***How often … ?* and adverbs of frequency** *How often do you clean your teeth?* *Do you ever get up late?* *always, often, sometimes, never* **Present simple with *always, often, sometimes, never*** *He sometimes watches TV.* *They never play tennis.* ***must/mustn't*** *What must I do?* *You mustn't wear your skates in the house.* *You must put them in the cupboard.*	***Let's be healthy!*** Learn about being safe when doing exercise and sports	***A bad, bad Monday morning*** A narrative Social and emotional skill: Thinking about the consequences of our actions	A1 Movers Reading and Writing Part 1
3 Party time! **Mission: Plan and act out a scene** Page 30	Jobs and parties Physical descriptions **Sounds and spelling:** /ɑ:/	**Present simple and present continuous** *I don't often listen to the radio.* *I'm not listening to it now.* ***Why … ?* and *Because …*** *Why are you asking a lot of questions?* *Because I love asking questions.*	***People who help us*** Learn about people who help us at home, at school and in the community	***The costume party*** A story Social and emotional skill: Asking for and offering help	A1 Movers Speaking Part 2
	Review units 1–3				
4 The family at home **Mission: Act out a visit to my cousins' new home** Page 44	Extended family In and around the home **Sounds and spelling:** /ʌ/	**Comparative adjectives with *-er*/*-ier* and *better*/*worse*** *My cousin's hair is longer/curlier than my uncle's.* *Shelly's singing is worse than Gracie's.* **Possessive pronouns** *Our car is smaller than my aunt and uncle's car, but ours is newer than theirs.*	***Machines in our homes*** Learn about machines at home and how they work	***Surprise!*** A story Social and emotional skill: Initiative and managing one's own emotions	A1 Movers Listening Part 3

Unit	Vocabulary	Grammar	Cross-curricular	Literature	Assessment
5 Animal world **Mission: Plan an animal documentary** Page 56	Wild and domestic animals Action verbs **Sounds and spelling:** *g*	**Superlative adjectives** *This kitten's the prettiest/the fattest.* *These ice skates are the best.* **Prepositions: *above*, *below*, *near*, *opposite*** *The bat's above the tree.* *The snail's below the flower.* *The parrot's near the cage.* *The bus stop's opposite the zoo.*	***The animal kingdom*** Learn about animals and their food	***Why the kangaroo has a pouch*** An Australian dreamtime story Social and emotional skill: Helping others	A1 Movers Reading and Writing Part 2
6 Our weather **Mission: Make a weather map for a country** Page 68	The weather Clothes **Sounds and spelling:** *ee* and *y*	***was/were*** *Were your grandparents here last weekend? Yes, they were.* *Were you at school on Tuesday? No, I wasn't.* ***There was / There were*** *Was there a scarf in the bedroom? Yes, there was.* *Were there any boots in the bedroom? No, there weren't.*	***What's the weather like today?*** Learn about instruments to measure the weather	***Fun in all types of weather!*** A poem Social and emotional skill: Thinking positively	A1 Movers Listening Part 1 and Part 2
	Review units 4–6				
7 Let's cook! **Mission: Make a class recipe book** Page 82	Food Actions in the kitchen **Sounds and spelling:** *ch*	**Past simple: irregular verbs** *I went swimming last Saturday.* *I didn't go shopping yesterday.* *Did you go to the park? Yes, I did.* **Past simple: regular verbs** *I liked cooking them!* *I fried the onions.* *I stopped because you started asking me questions.*	***Plants are delicious!*** Learn about how we use plants in food	***Sonny's dream job*** A fantasy story Social and emotional skill: Perseverance	A1 Movers Speaking Part 3
8 Around town **Mission: Write a trip review** Page 94	A day trip Places in town **Sounds and spelling:** *ow* and *oa*	**Past simple: more irregular verbs** *I found my old hat.* *He bought it last year.* ***have to / don't have to*** *I have to see the eye doctor at the hospital.* *My brother has to wear glasses.* *Do you have to wear glasses? Yes, I do.*	***Road safety*** Learn how to be safe in town	***Tom's first day on the school bus*** A fantasy story Social and emotional skill: Being optimistic	A1 Movers Listening Part 4
9 A big change **Mission: Plan a holiday world tour** Page 106	Adjectives for opinions and feelings A new adventure **Sounds and spelling:** *ing* or *in*	**Comparative adjectives with *more*** *Circus clothes are more beautiful than these.* *The circus is more exciting than the farm!* **Superlative adjectives with *most*** *This city is one of the most beautiful in the world.* *In my family, my brother is the most frightened of spiders.*	***The wonders of the world*** Learn about natural and manmade wonders of the world	***The mystery picnic*** A counting poem Social and emotional skill: Pride in your work	A1 Movers Reading and Writing Part 3
	Review units 7–9				

Meet the family

1 Read and write the words.

eight fine His live meet name ~~old~~

1

2

3

4

5

6

2 Listen and write. 4.07

Name: Jack

Family name: ________

Age: ________

House number: ________

Street: ________

Town: ________

The Friendly Farm

1 Listen and number. Then listen again and write.

4.08

a

b

c

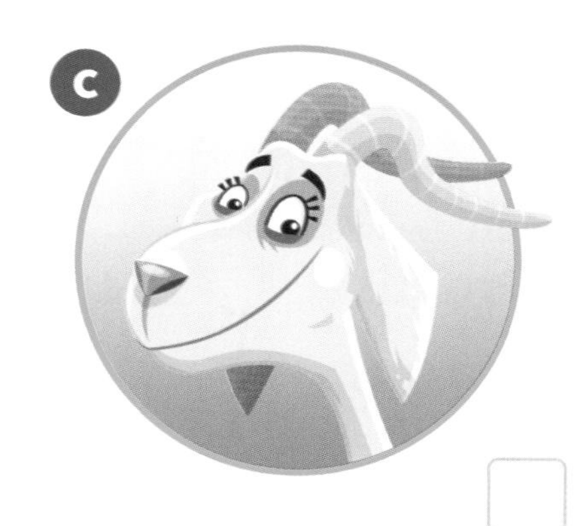

d

e

1

Cameron

f

2 Match. Draw lines with the right colour.

1 Is Harry's dad big? (black)
2 Is the photo of Shelly's brother? (blue)
3 Can Shelly sing? (red)
4 Is Rocky's mother asleep? (orange)
5 Does Gracie like eating paper? (pink)
6 Is Harry's dad sad? (purple)
7 Does Cameron like Shelly's singing? (green)

a Yes, she does.
b Yes, she is.
c Yes, he is.
d No, he doesn't.
e No, he isn't.
f No, she can't.
g No, it isn't.

1 A day on the farm

My unit goals

Practise	Say and write	Learn to say
 	 8 10 12 new words in English	in English

My mission diary

	Hooray!	OK	Try again

My favourite stage: ___________

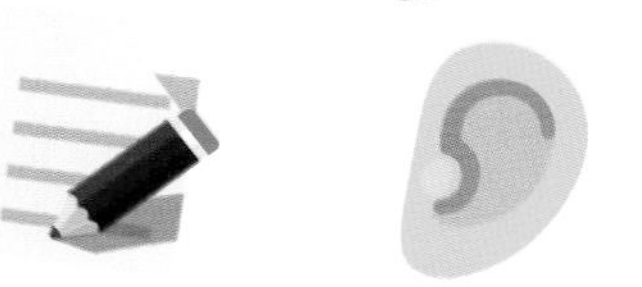

Go to page 120 and add to your word stack!

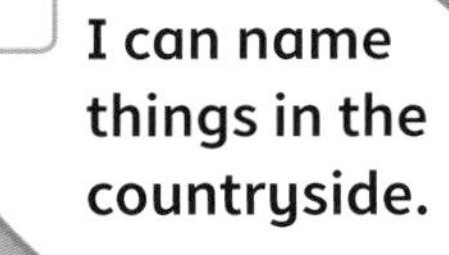
I can name things in the countryside.

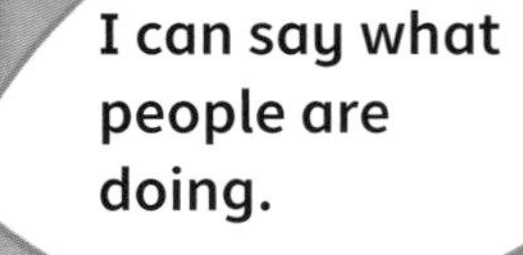
I can say what people are doing.

I can write about my daily routines.

I can say what's different in two pictures.

1 Read and match.

a 

b 

c 

d  1

e 

f 

g 

h 

1 Vicky and Charlie are sitting next to the lake.

2 It's a nice day. Let's go for a walk in the forest.

3 Jane's fishing in the river with her grandma.

4 Look at those cows in that field.

5 Lily and Jack are playing on the grass.

6 There are a lot of brown leaves under that tree.

7 My dog is digging in the ground.

8 There's a big mountain behind Fred's house.

Sounds and spelling

2 4.09 Listen and circle the words with a /r/ sound. Then listen again and match.

a leaf [ ]

b river [ ]

c rock [ ]

d grass [ ]

e tractor [1]

f field [ ]

1 Listen and circle the correct words. 1.10

1. Rocky's *talking* / *singing* to Cameron and Henrietta.
2. The kittens *are* / *aren't* sleeping.
3. The mother cat's washing the kitten's *legs* / *face*.
4. The puppy with the short tail is *playing* / *eating*.
5. The big puppy's looking at its *tail* / *face*.
6. The fat puppy's *eating* / *washing* the red sock.

2 Talk about the pictures. Use the words from the box.

drinking eating looking playing sleeping

Look at the fat puppy. It's eating a red sock.

1 Read and match. Colour.

1 Fred's eating

3 Vicky's mum's taking

their shoes.

a photo.

2 Daisy's washing

4 Mary and Paul are cleaning

her face.

an ice cream.

2 Answer the questions.

1 

Are the puppies sleeping?

No, they aren't.

2 

Is the kitten playing?

3 

Is the girl eating sausages?

4 

Are the children walking?

5 

Is the boy washing his hands?

6 

Is the bird singing?

7 

Is the woman putting on her shoes?

8 

Is the man driving a car?

1 Write the words. Find the secret word.

1 He **tegs** gets up at eight o'clock.

2 She has a **wesohr** ____________ in the evening.

3 I put **ttthpsaeoo** ____________ on my toothbrush.

4 I clean my **hetet** ____________ at night.

5 My dad **sha** ____________ a shower in the evening.

6 I have **asefatrkb** ____________ at nine o'clock. I eat bread and milk.

7 I get **redseds** ____________ in the morning.

8 I love chicken and rice for **chlnu** ____________.

9 My mum **skwea** ____________ up at seven o'clock.

10 My sister **sshewa** ____________ her hands at lunch.

1 g e t s
2
3
4
5
6
7
8
9
10

What's the secret word?

____

2 Listen and tick ✓.

4.10

1 What's the kitten doing?

a b c

2 What's Peter doing now?

a 

b 

c 

3 What colour is Charlie's toothbrush?

a 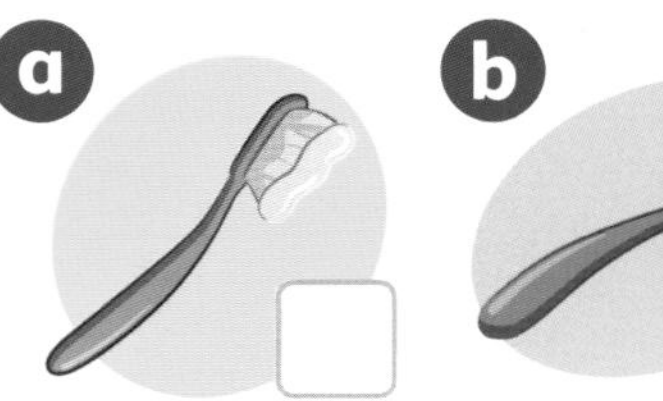

b 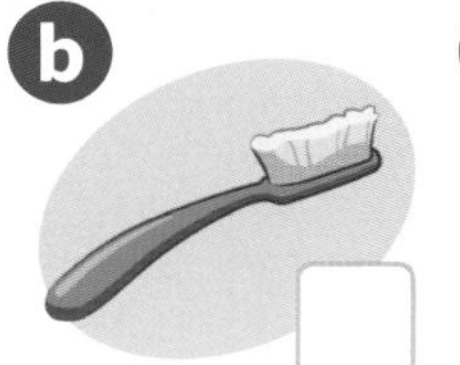

c 

4 What does Daisy have for breakfast today?

a 

b 

c 

1 Write the words in the correct order.

1 at seven / wakes up / Jack / o'clock / .

Jack wakes up at seven o'clock.

2 Do the / dinner with / their family / children have / ?

____

3 school / have / Jim doesn't / lunch at / .

____

4 Sally have / Does / her mum / breakfast with / ?

____

5 school at / nine o'clock / Mary / goes to / .

____

6 Charlie clean / the bathroom / their teeth in / Peter and / .

____

2 Read and write the words.

breakfast cleans dressed gets has o'clock ~~up~~ walks

Vicky wakes 1 ___up___ at seven o'clock every day. She 2 __________ up and goes to the bathroom. She 3 __________ a shower and gets 4 __________ . She has 5 __________ with her dad in the kitchen. Then she 6 __________ her teeth and goes to school. She 7 __________ to school with her mum. School starts at nine 8 __________ . Vicky loves school.

1 Tick ✓ the things that are good for the Earth.

1

2
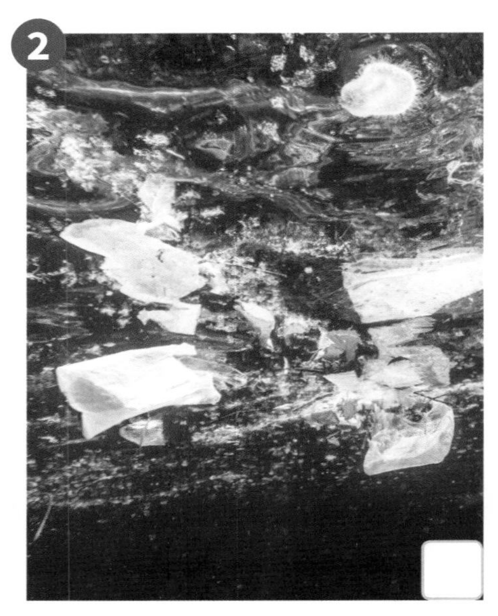

3

4

5

6

2 Read and write *yes* or *no*.

1 People can live on all the planets in our solar system. no

2 We can live on Earth because there is water and air. ______

3 Living things need plastic to live. ______

4 Dirty air and water are bad for the planet and for us. ______

5 Everybody must help look after the planet. ______

3 Which is better for the Earth? Look and tick ✓.

4 How can we look after the planet? Draw and write.

1 Read and circle the correct answer.

1 Where are Beth and Gwen? a at home b at school
2 Who do they go to see? a a dog called Jess b a friend called Jess
3 Where does the dog play? a in the kitchen b in the field
4 Who falls over? a Beth b Gwen
5 Why does Gwen stop running? a she wins the race b to help her sister

2 Read the sentences. Write *yes* or *no*. Explain your answers.

1 Beth wants to see Jess.

yes The poem says, 'Come on, Gwen!' says Beth. 'Let's go and see Jess!'

2 Jess is an old dog.

3 Beth and Gwen see Jess every day.

4 Beth falls on the ground.

5 Gwen doesn't help her sister.

3 What do you enjoy doing with your family? Write, then talk with a friend.

I like

I like going swimming with my family!

Listen and draw lines.

Kim Sally Peter Mary

John Lily Nick

1 4.12 Find four differences.

1 Play the game.

What's this? It's a toothbrush.

HAVE ANOTHER TURN

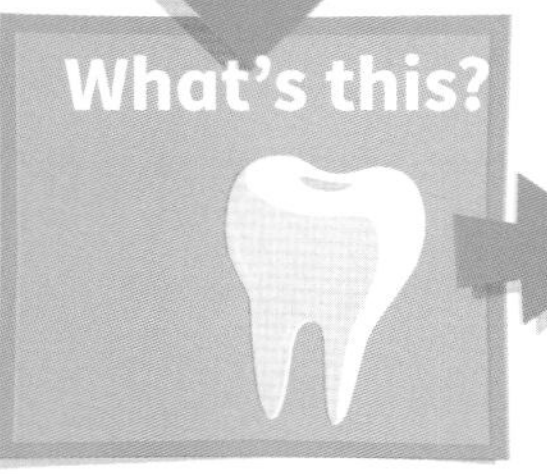

HAVE ANOTHER TURN

INSTRUCTIONS

1 Roll the dice and move your counter.

2 Answer the question.

2 My week

My unit goals

Practise

Say and write

8 10 12

new words in English

Learn to say

in English

My mission diary

	Hooray!	OK	Try again
 1			
 2			
 3			

My favourite stage: ___________

Go to page 120 and add to your word stack!

- [ ] I can name the days of the week.
- [ ] I can ask and answer questions with *How often ...?*
- [ ] I can talk about free time activities.
- [ ] I can read sentences and copy English words.

1 Read and write the words.

Friday ~~Monday~~ Saturday Sunday
Thursday Tuesday Wednesday weekend

1 Sunday comes between Saturday and ___Monday___.
2 Friday comes after ______________.
3 Tuesday comes before ______________.
4 Thursday comes between Wednesday and ______________.
5 Monday comes before ______________.
6 Saturday and Sunday are the ______________.
7 Monday comes after ______________.
8 The weekend is ______________ and Sunday.

Sounds and spelling

2 Listen and say the rhyme.

4.13

On Monday and Tuesday,
I don't play.

On Wednesday and
Thursday, I do.

On Friday and Saturday,
I play all day.

On Sunday, I play at
the zoo!

1 Listen and complete the sentences.

1.24

1 Let's put Fred here on the table.

2 Jim and Jenny have got a ______________.

3 How often do they ______________?

4 How often does it wash ______________?

5 I don't know. No, I don't ______________.

6 I sometimes talk, but I never talk ______________!

2 Circle the word that is true for you. Write, then tell your friend.

1 I *sometimes* / *always* / *never* play tennis at the weekend.

2 I *sometimes* / *always* / *never* do my homework at school.

3 I *sometimes* / *always* / *never* watch TV on Wednesdays.

4 I sometimes ______________________________.

5 I always ______________________________.

6 I never ______________________________.

I sometimes play tennis at the weekend.

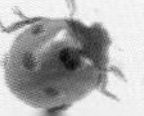

1 Read and write the words.

before ~~called~~ evening kitten never plays sometimes

Vicky's got a new kitten. He's 1 called Simba. Vicky always feeds him 2 ______ breakfast in the morning and after dinner in the 3 ______ . She often 4 ______ with him before school. They love playing. Simba likes sleeping in the sun. He often sleeps in the garden, but when there's no sun he 5 ______ sleeps in his bed in the living room. He's 6 ______ naughty – he's a very good 7 ______ .

2 Join and write the sentences.

1 She doesn't	never eats	he play	before lunch.
2 They always	our	their	every day.
3 How often	wash	listen to	homework after school?
4 She	often	their hands	for breakfast.
5 We feed	does	burgers	in the park?
6 Do they	always do	puppy twice	the radio.

1 She doesn't often listen to the radio.

2 ______

3 ______

4 ______

5 ______

6 ______

1 Look and write the words.

go shopping · go skating · ~~listen to a CD~~ · listen to music · read a comic · watch a DVD · watch films · write an email

1 

listen to a CD

2 

______

3 

______

4 

______

5 

______

6 

______

7 

______

8 

______

2 Look at the pictures in Activity 1. Complete the sentences.

1 When I do my homework I never listen to music on the radio.

2 Every Saturday, May ______ a film at the cinema with her mum.

3 Jane enjoys reading ______. Her mum buys her favourite one every Friday afternoon.

4 We ______ in town every weekend to buy things.

5 I never listen to music on the radio. I always ______ a CD in my bedroom.

6 We like to take our skates and ______ in the park.

7 I sometimes write an ______ to my cousin. He lives in a different town.

8 I never go to the cinema. I watch ______ at home.

1 Read and write the words.

Sally enjoys reading comics. She gets a new 1 ___comic___ every Saturday morning and she reads it in her 2 ________ before lunch. She goes shopping with her 3 ________ every Saturday afternoon. They always go to the same 4 ________ to buy their fruit. Today they're buying 5 ________. Sally's very happy. They're her favourite fruit.

books

bedroom

~~comic~~

dad

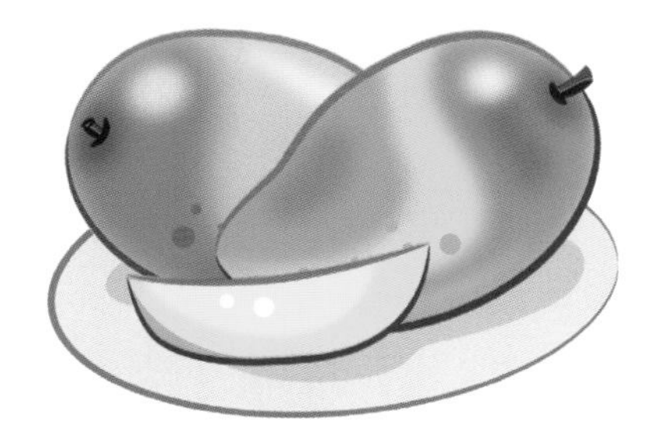

mangoes

shop

2 Read and match.

1	You must study	a	her homework after school.
2	What must we take	b	his dirty shoes on the sofa.
3	He mustn't put	c	my helmet when I roller skate.
4	They mustn't eat	d	for your tests.
5	She must do	e	our hands before lunch.
6	We must always wash	f	when we go shopping?
7	I must remember	g	sweets in the lesson.

1 Draw the things that are missing in the picture.

2 Read and write the names.

1

Daisy

2

3

4

5

6

Sally is wearing gloves and a helmet. Nick has got goggles and a towel. Jane is wearing goggles, gloves and a helmet. Charlie is wearing gloves. Daisy is wearing a helmet and gloves. John is wearing a helmet, knee pads and elbow pads.

3 Write.

When I ____________________ I wear ______________________________.

4 Who is looking after their bodies? Look and tick ✓.

5 Complete the sentences with the words from the box.

clothes drink helmet ~~muscles~~ sun cream water

1 It is important to warm up our muscles before we exercise.

2 When we get hot, our body loses ________. So it's important to ________ lots when we do sport.

3 We must use ________ to protect our skin from the sun.

4 It is important to wear the correct ________ when we do sport.

5 We must wear a ________ when we ride a bike or go skating.

1 Read the story again. Complete the notes.

Name of the story: A bad, bad Monday morning

Main character

Name: ____________________

What's he like? ____________________

How do you know? ____________________

Where and when?

At the beginning: ____________________

In the middle: ____________________

At the end: ____________________

2 Tick ✓ the best answer.

The story is about:

a Alex's presentation at school. ☐

b What happens when Alex doesn't get up on time. ☐

c Alex's favourite day of the week. ☐

3 Can you think of ways to help Alex with his problem?

____

____

Listen and tick ✓.

1 When are the football matches?

a OCTOBER

M	T	W	T	F	S	S
1	2	(3)	4	5	6	7
8	9	(10)	11	12	13	14
15	16	(17)	18	19	20	21
22	23	(24)	25	26	27	
29	30	(31)				

b OCTOBER ✓

M	T	W	T	F	S	S
1	2	3	4	5	(6)	7
8	9	10	11	12	(13)	14
15	16	17	18	19	(20)	21
22	23	24	25	26	(27)	
29	30	31				

c OCTOBER

M	T	W	T	F	S	S
(1)	2	3	4	5	6	7
(8)	9	10	11	12	13	14
(15)	16	17	18	19	20	21
(22)	23	24	25	26	27	
(29)	30	31				

2 What does the boy want?

a 

b 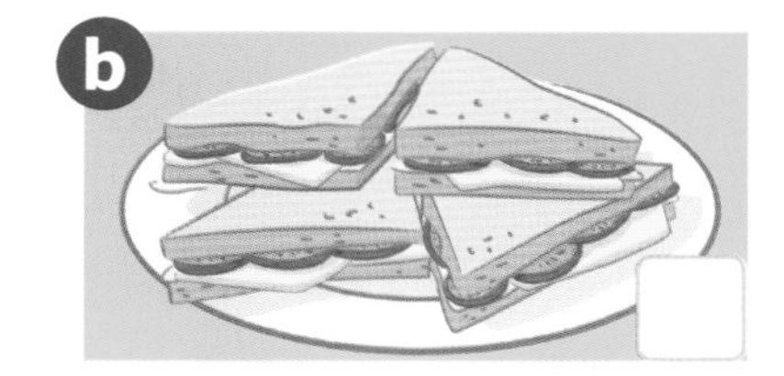

c 

3 What does the boy want to do?

a 

b 

c 

4 Who is the girl's PE teacher?

a 

b 

c 

5 Where are the children?

a 

b 

c 

6 What is the boy looking for?

a 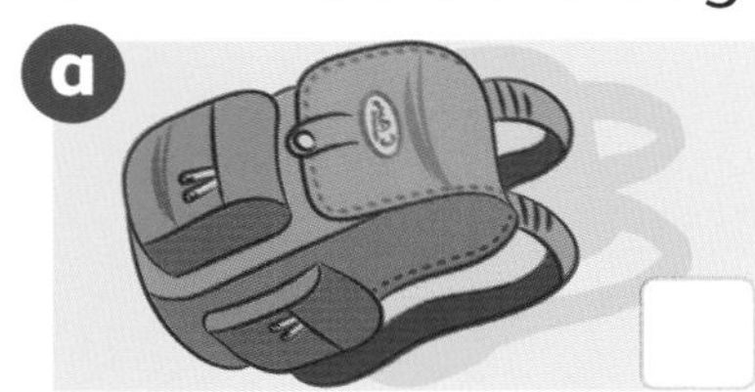

b 

c 

1 Look and read. Choose the correct words and write them on the lines. There is one example.

an email

films

rocks

a forest

a comic book

grass

a lake

roller skating

Example

Lizards like to sit on these when the sun is out. rocks

Questions

1 You find this in the garden on the ground. ________

2 Some people write this on a computer. ________

3 There are lots of trees in this place. ________

4 You can watch these at home on your TV. ________

5 This is in the countryside and you often see fish here. ________

1 Play the game.

I always read comics on Saturdays.

INSTRUCTIONS

1 Look at the words and pictures and write four sentences.
2 Roll the dice and move your counter.
3 Collect your words.
4 Say your sentences.

Party time!

My unit goals

Practise

Say and write

new words in English

Learn to say

in English

My mission diary

	Hooray!	OK	Try again

My favourite stage: ______________

Go to page 120 and add to your word stack!

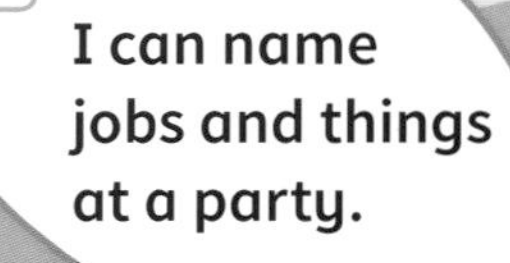

- [ ] I can name jobs and things at a party.
- [ ] I can talk about what people look like.
- [ ] I can ask and answer questions with *Why … ?* and *Because …*
- [ ] I can use pictures to tell a story.

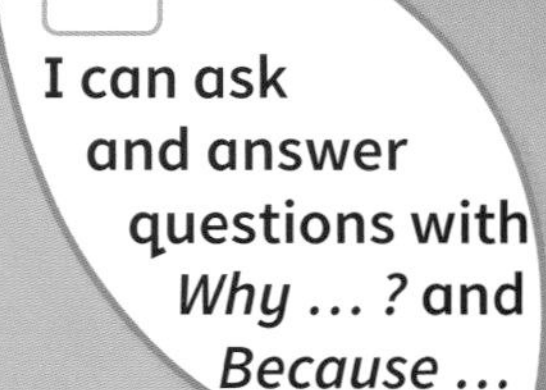

1 Write the words. Find the secret word.

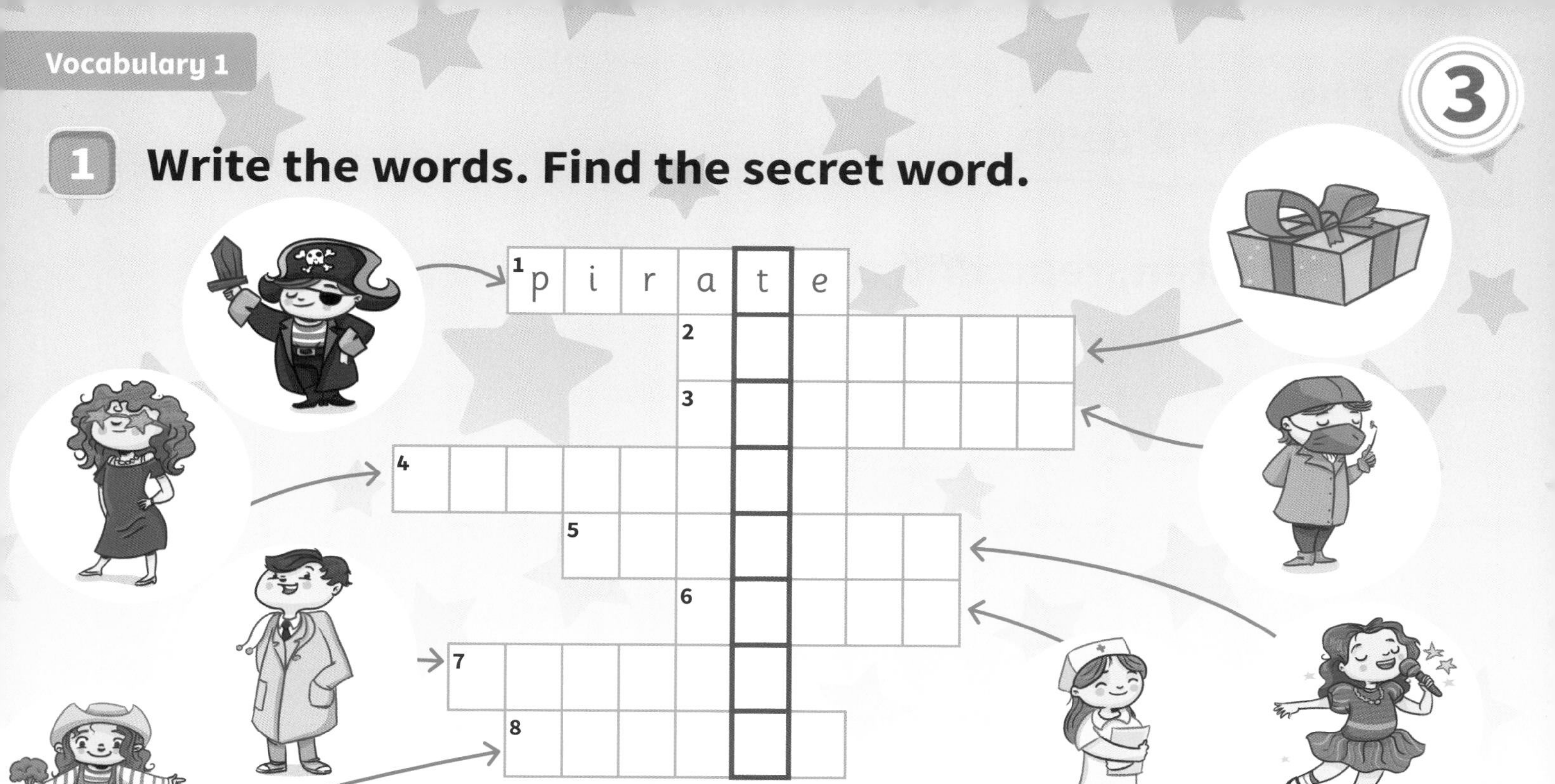

What is the secret word? ______________________

Sounds and spelling

2 4.15 **Can you hear the /a:/ sound? Listen and say *yes* or *no*.**

3 4.16 **Listen and colour the letters that make the /a:/ sound.**

father
grandpa
grandma

1 1.38 Listen, read and correct.

1 Cameron's wearing a ~~dentist's~~ costume from the party. clown's
2 Farmer Friendly's outside feeding the sheep. ______
3 Shelly wants to be a pop star. ______
4 Gracie likes studying. She can be a pirate. ______
5 Doctors help other clowns. ______
6 Gracie wants to look at Harry's hat. ______

2 Read and write the words.

~~feeding~~ helping wants wear

1 Grandpa always feeds the cows in the evening. He's feeding them now.
2 Cameron's wearing a clown's costume. He doesn't often ______ clothes.
3 Doctors always help people. Gracie's ______ Harry.
4 Film stars often go to parties. Shelly ______ to be a film star.

1 Read and circle the correct words.

1 It's eight o'clock now. Charlie *is having* / *has* a shower.

2 Vicky *is having* / *has* dinner at eight o'clock every day.

3 Jim and Daisy often *are playing* / *play* tennis at the weekend.

4 Sally never *is wearing* / *wears* a dress.

5 Fred's in the bathroom. He *'s washing* / *washes* his face.

6 Mary and Jane sometimes *are skating* / *skate* in the park after school.

7 It's bedtime. Peter *'s getting* / *gets* undressed.

8 Vicky loves swimming. She always *is going* / *goes* for a swim on Saturdays.

2 Read and write the names.

1 ________ 2 ________ 3 ________ 4 Jim

My dad never watches TV in the morning, he makes my breakfast. He's called Jim and he's making my breakfast now.

My friend's got a fish. She feeds it every morning. She isn't feeding it now. She's skateboarding. Her name's Vicky.

My brother always wears jeans and a T-shirt at the weekend, but today he's at a party. He's wearing a dentist's costume. His name's Paul.

My sister Lily loves skateboarding, but she isn't skateboarding now. She's doing her homework.

1 Listen and number. 4.17

a 

b 

c  1

d 

e 

f 

2 Look, read and write.

Complete the sentences.

1 The pirate's got a long, black ______beard______.

2 The tall clown's got purple, curly ____________.

Answer the questions.

3 What's the boy with the straight, blond hair? ____________

4 What are the clowns doing? ____________

5 Now write a sentence about the picture.

____

1 Write the words in the correct order.

1 cleaning / his teeth / Why's / he / ?
Why's he cleaning his teeth?

2 a film star / I'm taking / because she's / photos of her / .

____

3 tennis because / They can't play / got a ball / they haven't / .

____

4 She's wearing / because she's / a helmet / riding a horse / .

____

5 happy today / because it's / Peter's very / his birthday / .

____

6 a party / wearing costumes / because they're at / They're / .

____

2 Match the questions with the answers.

1 Why's he getting his swimsuit and towel?
2 Why aren't the children at school?
3 Why's she wearing a helmet?
4 Why's he writing an email to his friends?
5 Why's she cleaning her shoes?

a Because they're dirty.
b Because she's roller skating.
c Because it's Tuesday. He always goes for a swim on Tuesdays.
d Because it's the weekend and they haven't got classes.
e Because he's inviting them to his party.

1 Write the words.

1 

t e a c h e r

2 

_ _ _ _ _ _ _ _ _ _ _ _ _

3 

_ _ _ _ _ _

4 

_ _ _ _ _

5 

_ _ _ _ _ _ _ _ _ _ _

6 

_ _ _ _ _ _ _

2 Look, read and match.

1	He's	a	in a hospital.
2	He works	b	sick children.
3	He wears	c	a nurse.
4	He looks after	d	a blue uniform.
5	She's a	e	traffic.
6	She works	f	police officer.
7	She wears	g	in a police station.
8	She controls the	h	a black uniform.

3 Who can help? Look and write the words.

1

police officer

2

3

4

4 Read and write the words.

dentist ~~doctor~~ farmer firefighter police officer teacher

1 This person looks after people in hospital. doctor

2 This person controls the traffic. ______

3 This person stops fires. ______

4 This person teaches children. ______

5 This person checks your teeth. ______

6 This person works with animals and plants. ______

1 Answer the questions.

1. Who's having a costume party? Why?

   Emily's having a costume party because it's her birthday.

2. What costume does Matt want?

   Matt really wants a ________ costume.

3. Why does his mother think a pirate costume is a good idea?

   Matt can make a beard and he's got a pirate ________.

4. What is Matt's costume in the end?

   It's a ________.

2 Complete the sentences.

beard ~~costume~~ funny pirate pop superhero

1. Everyone needs a costume for Emily's party.
2. Harry has a ________ costume for the party, but he can't fly!
3. Matt can make a ________ and a moustache.
4. He has a ________ hat.
5. Emily sings because she is a ________ star at her party.
6. Everyone laughs at Matt's costume because he looks very ________.

3 Ask your friends for ideas, then draw your costume for Emily's party in your notebook.

Can you help me think of a costume for the party?

What about a ________?

Look, read and write.

a party

a farmer

~~a superhero~~

a sheep

a hat

a moustache

1. This person is in comics and on TV and films. a superhero
2. People wear this on their heads. ______
3. You have this when it's your birthday. ______
4. This person keeps animals or grows vegetables, cereals or fruit. ______
5. This animal has a thick, white, curly coat. ______

1 4.18 Tell the story.

Mary and Zoe are pop stars.

1 Play the game.

INSTRUCTIONS

1 Roll the dice and move your counter.
2 Describe the person.

The farmer's tall. He's got fair hair and a moustache.

Review Units 1–3

1 Listen and draw lines. 4.19

1 
2 
3 
4 
5 

Monday Tuesday Wednesday Thursday Friday

2 Circle the odd one out. Say why.

1	Tuesday	Wednesday	Friday	weekend
2	clown	watch a film	listen to music	go skating
3	toothpaste	toothbrush	bed	towel
4	farm	sea	lake	river
5	pirate	present	film star	dentist
6	curly	straight	blonde	fat
7	go to bed	wake up	get dressed	have breakfast

Weekend is different.

Why?

Because it's not a day.

3 Look and read. Write *yes* or *no*.

1 A kitten is eating flowers. no

2 A farmer is wearing dirty boots in the house. ______

3 A fat puppy is eating a toothbrush. ______

4 A fat puppy is sleeping on the television. ______

5 A pirate is eating lunch with clean hands. ______

6 A cook is walking on the table. ______

7 A nurse is riding a bike. ______

4 Look at the picture in Activity 3 and complete the sentences. Use *must*/*mustn't* and a word from the box.

eat (x2) have ~~sleep~~ walk wear (x2)

1 The fat puppy mustn't sleep on the television.

2 The farmer ______ dirty boots in the house.

3 The thin puppy ______ the toothbrush.

4 The puppy ______ the flowers.

5 The boy ______ clean hands when he eats his lunch.

6 The orange kitten ______ on the table.

7 The girl ______ a helmet when she rides her bike.

4 The family at home

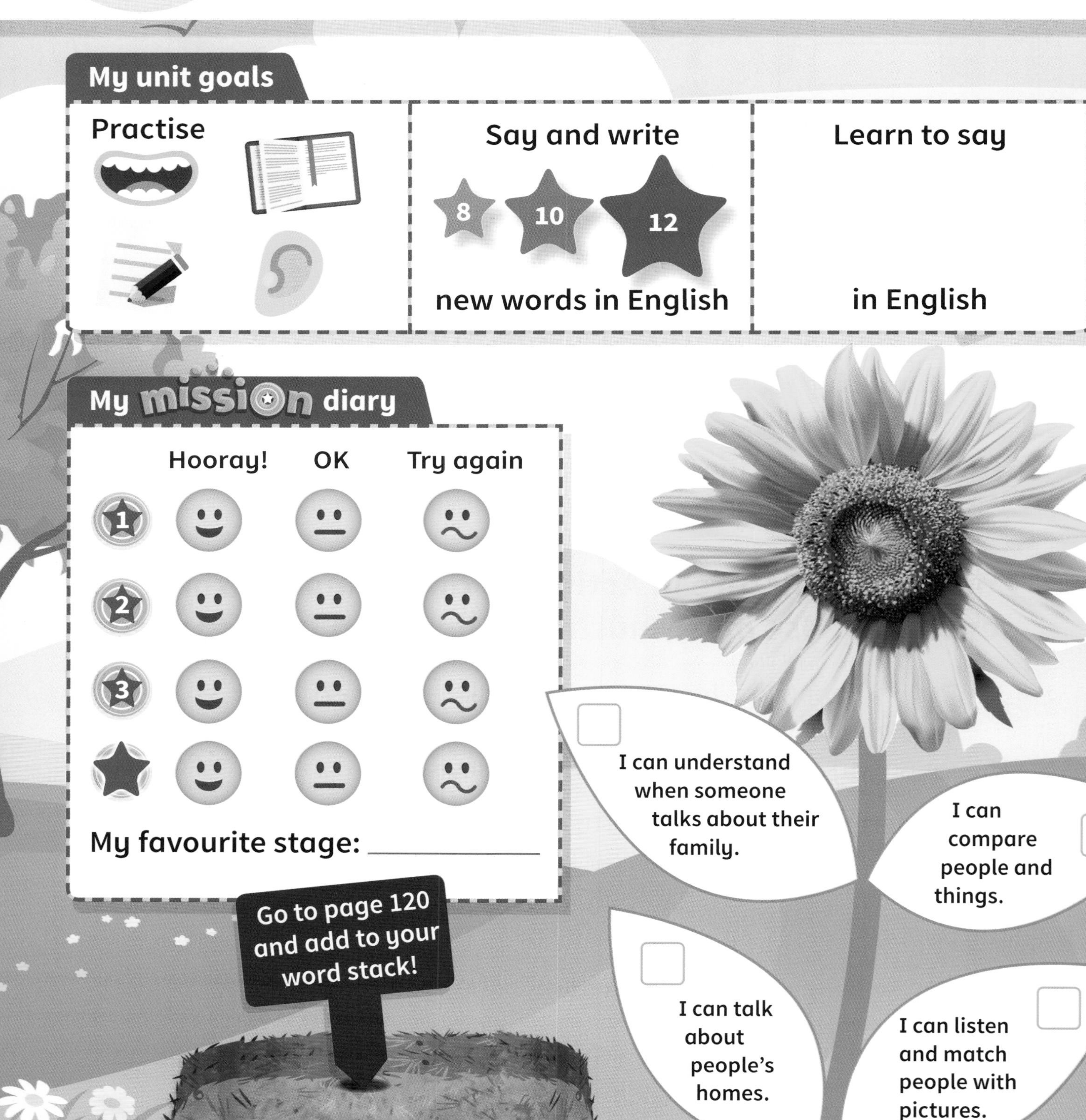

1 Write the words.

1 Zoe is Jim and Jenny's **nicsou** cousin .
2 Jack is Jim and Jenny's **lecnu** ________ .
3 Jenny is Mr Friendly's **ghtaured** ________ .
4 Jim is Mrs Friendly's **nso** ________ .
5 Julia is Jim and Jenny's **tuna** ________ .
6 Jim is Grandma Friendly's **snogradn** ________ .
7 Jenny is Grandpa Friendly's **rddtganuergha** ________ .
8 Mr and Mrs Friendly are Jim and Jenny's **snetrap** ________ .
9 Grandma and Grandpa Friendly are Zoe's **strapnendrag** ________ .

Sounds and spelling

How do we write that sound?

2 4.20 Can you hear the /ʌ/ sound? Listen and say *yes* or *no*.

3 4.21 Listen and colour the letters that make the /ʌ/ sound.

mother
brother son

mum
uncle

cousin

1 Listen, read and tick ✓ or cross ✗.

2.02

1. It's funnier than the family photo in the living room. ✓
2. Jim and Jenny's uncle is shorter than their dad. ☐
3. Jim and Jenny's cousin is bigger and older than them. ☐
4. Gracie's ears are shorter than Shelly's. ☐
5. Shelly's feet are smaller and cleaner than Gracie's. ☐
6. The animals must all be nicer to everyone. ☐

2 Write sentences. Talk with your friends.

bigger   older   prettier   smaller   thinner   younger

Rocky's younger than Henrietta.

1 Write the comparatives.

~~angry~~ ~~bad~~ ~~big~~ curly fat good happy ~~long~~ naughty
sad short straight tall thin ugly young

+er	~~y~~ +ier	double letter +er	irregular
longer	angrier	bigger	worse
______	______	______	______
______	______	______	
______	______	______	
______	______		

2 Join and write the sentences.

1 My mum's hair's	are thinner	better than	dog's tail.
2 The cat's tail's	beard's shorter	than my uncle's	our old one.
3 The kittens	curlier than	than the	beard.
4 My dad's	house is	than	aunt's hair.
5 Our new	longer	my	the puppies.

1 My mum's hair's curlier than my aunt's hair.

2 ______

3 ______

4 ______

5 ______

Vocabulary 2 and song

1  Circle the odd one out. Say why.

A village is not part of your house.

1	basement	roof	(village)	balcony
2	clown	first floor	dentist	nurse
3	city	stairs	village	town
4	doctor	second floor	first floor	third floor
5	lake	field	basement	river
6	straight	curly	roof	fair
7	beard	village	moustache	hair
8	son	daughter	parents	balcony
9	basement	present	cake	costume
10	film	DVD	TV	downstairs

2 4.22 Listen and write a letter in each box.

his aunt

c

his uncle

his grandparents

his parents

a

b

c

d

1 Read and match. Colour.

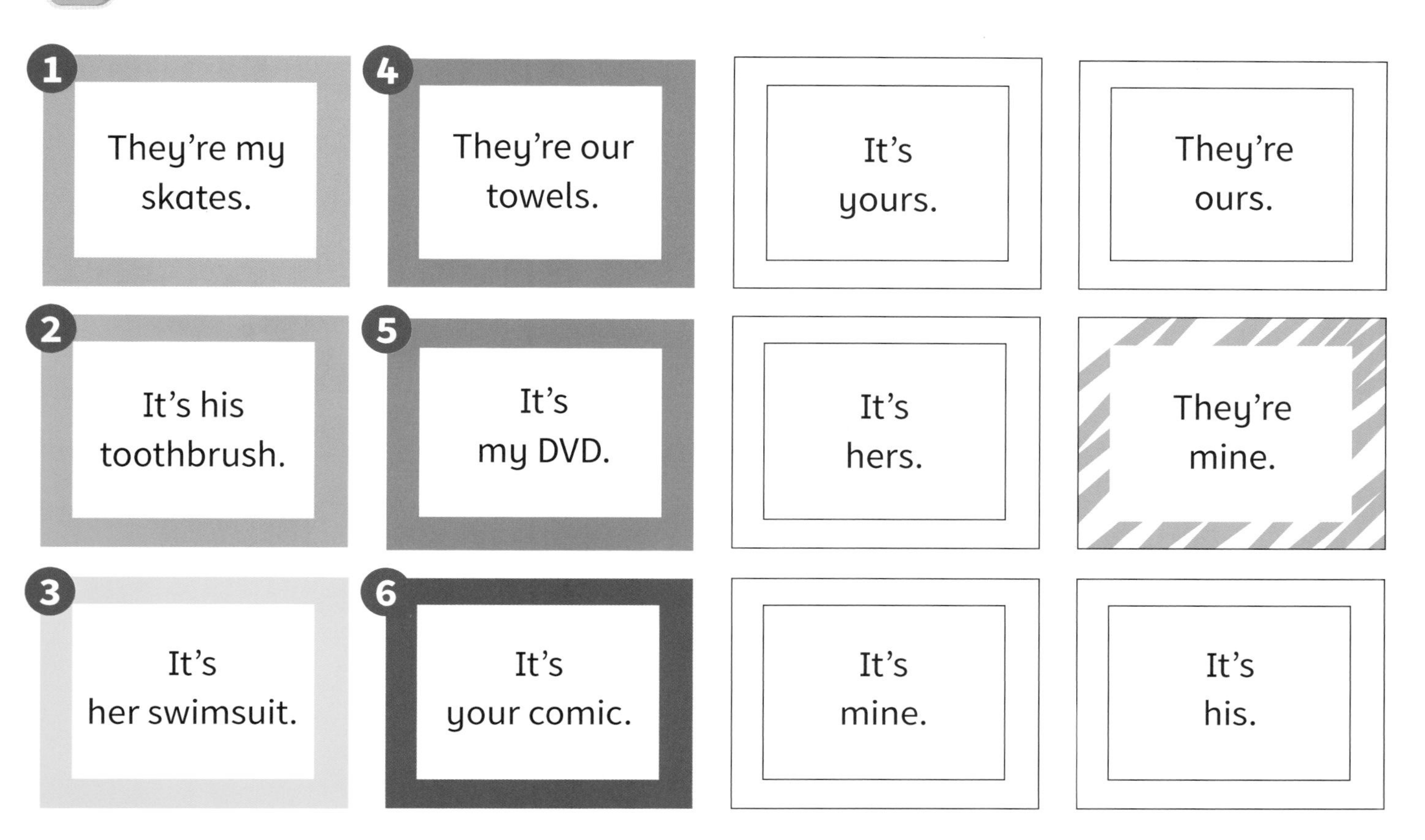

2 Read and circle the correct words.

1 A Is that your grandpa's tractor?

B Yes, it's *his* / *hers*.

2 A Vicky, Jane, where are your shoes?

B *Mine* / *Theirs* are next to the stairs and *his* / *hers* are in the cupboard.

3 A Is that the pirates' treasure?

B Yes, it's *theirs* / *mine*.

4 A Are these CDs yours or your dad's?

B They're *his* / *hers*.

5 A Is this book mine or yours?

B It's *his* / *yours*.

1 Look and match the machine with the problem.

2 Where do we use these machines? Write the words.

in the house   in the classroom   in the street   in the park

1 in the house
2 ______
3 ______
4 ______

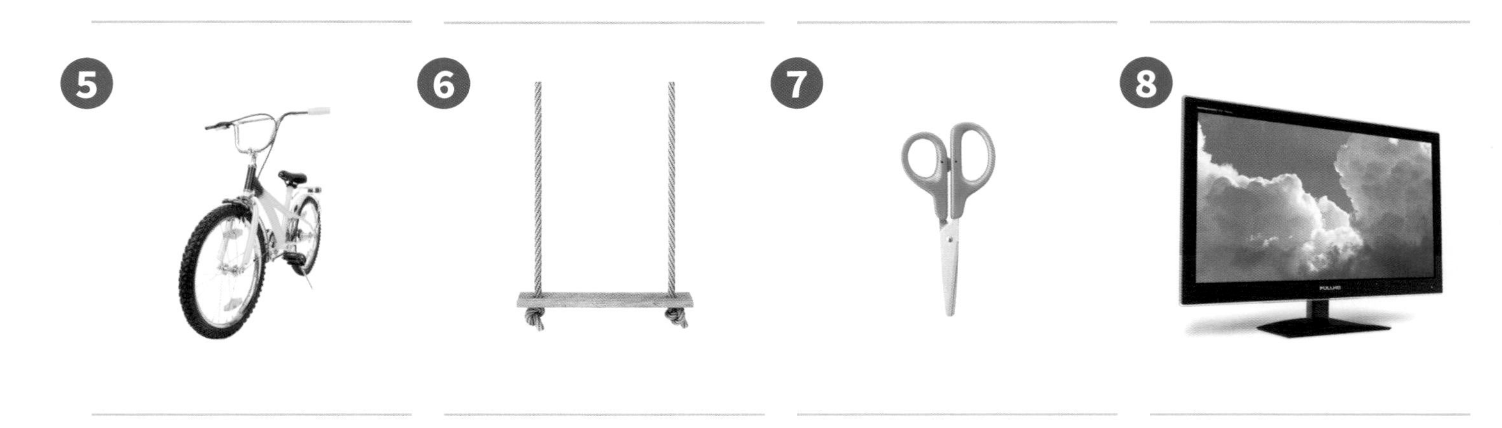

5 ______
6 ______
7 ______
8 ______

3 Look at Activity 4. Number the photos.

a 

b 

c 

d 

e 

f 

g 

h 

4 Do you help at home? Put a tick ✓ or cross ✗. Then ask your friends.

		You	______	______	______
1	Do you lay the table?				
2	Do you wash the dishes or fill the dishwasher?				
3	Do you make your bed?				
4	Do you tidy your room?				
5	Do you water the plants?				
6	Do you help your parents cook?				
7	Do you vacuum the floor?				
8	Do you load the washing machine?				

Do you lay the table?

Yes, I do.

1 Answer the questions.

1 Whose birthday is it?

It's Max's mum's birthday.

2 What food is there at the party?

____

3 Why are Uncle Paul and Grandma on the balcony?

____

4 Why is Max's mum late?

____

5 What idea does Max have?

____

2 Write the words. Act it out with a friend.

~~Mum~~ party phone train

Max: Where is 1 Mum ?

Uncle Paul: I don't know, Max.

Max: She's very late. We can't have the 2 ________ without her.

Uncle Paul: Is she on the 3 ________ home?

Max: Maybe.

Uncle Paul: Max! That's the 4 ________ ! Quick!

3 What do you do for your birthday? Do you have a big party? Tell your friend.

I like watching DVDs with my friends and then having a big party at home!

Look, read and write.

1 Mum is wearing a green ____hat____.

2 Marta and Juan are reading ________________.

3 Uncle Paul is drinking some ________________.

4 What is Max's dad wearing?

____

5 Where is the football?

____

6 What is Max doing?

____

7 Now write two sentences about the picture.

____

____

1 4.23 **Lily is telling her teacher about different people in her family and where they live. Which is each person's home? Listen and write a letter in each box. There is one example.**

her brother

her grandfather

her cousin

her uncle

her aunt

her grandmother

A

B

C

D

E

F

G

H
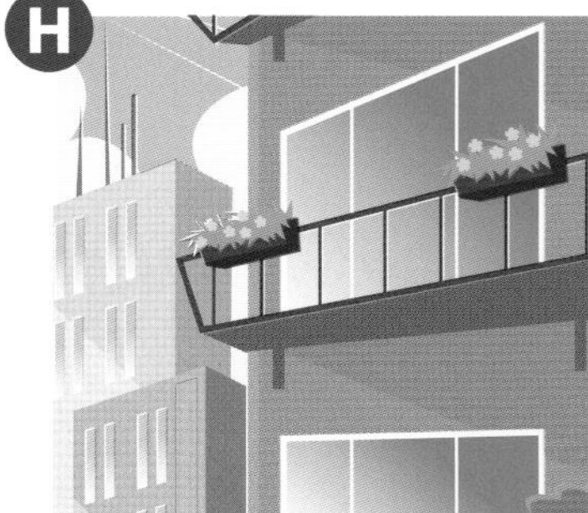

1 Play the game.

It's time for lunch. Go to the dining room.

You help your grandparents make lunch. Go to the kitchen.

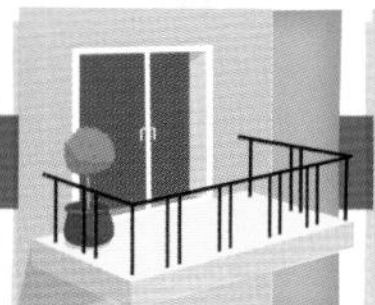

Go to the stairs and help your younger cousin go up them.

You want to clean your teeth. Go to the bathroom.

There's a cat asleep on a roof!

Go upstairs to your bedroom.

Today you can play outside. Go to the garden.

Go downstairs to the basement.

Which places are you going to?

balcony	☐
basement	☐
bathroom	☐
bedroom	☐
dining room	☐
garden	☐
hall	☐
kitchen	☐
living room	☐
roof	☐
stairs	☐
street	☐

Go shopping in the city with your parents.

Your uncle is on the balcony. Go and talk to him.

You want to watch TV. Go to the living room.

Your aunt's here. Go to the hall to open the door.

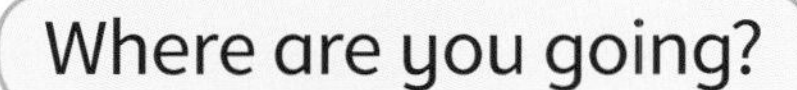

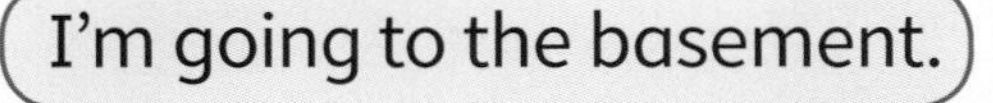

INSTRUCTIONS

1 Choose a place to start.
2 Tick four places on your list.
3 Roll the dice and move your counter.
4 Visit the places on your list.

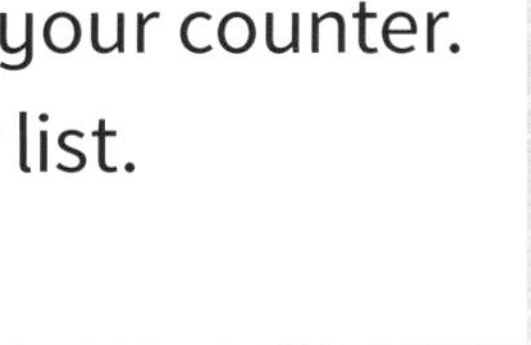

Animal world

My unit goals

Practise	Say and write	Learn to say
   	 8 10 12 new words in English	in English

My mission diary

	Hooray!	OK	Try again

My favourite stage: ___________

Go to page 120 and add to your word stack!

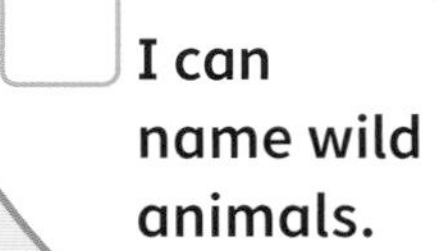

- [ ] I can name wild animals.
- [ ] I can talk about things animals do.
- [ ] I can use words like *above* to say where things are.
- [ ] I can choose the best answers in a conversation.

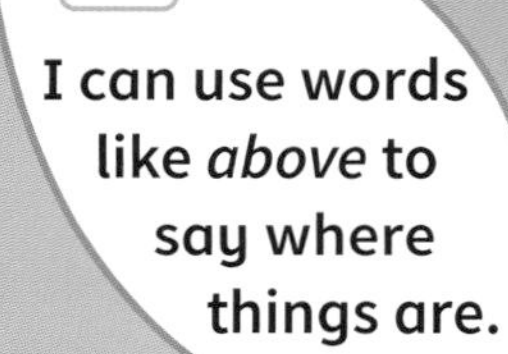

1 Read and match.

bat bear dolphin kangaroo lion panda
parrot ~~penguin~~ rabbit whale

1 This black and white bird can't fly. penguin
2 This clever animal lives in the sea. It's got a long nose and mouth. ______
3 This small animal sleeps under the ground and jumps a lot. ______
4 This small black and brown animal can fly, but it isn't a bird. ______
5 This is a very big cat. It likes eating and sleeping. ______
6 This beautiful bird's got a lot of colours. Sometimes it can speak. ______
7 This big brown and black animal can climb trees and swim. ______
8 This big animal's got long legs and short arms. It jumps a lot. ______
9 This black and white bear doesn't eat meat, it eats leaves. ______
10 This grey or black animal is bigger than all other sea animals. ______

Sounds and spelling

2 Listen and say. Then listen and match.

4.24

1 Listen, read and circle the correct words. 2.19

1 Jim's picture is of a *wildlife* / *car* park.
2 The bear's *the biggest* / *the smallest*.
3 The kangaroo's *nose* / *tail* is longer than Harry's.
4 Shelly thinks the *parrot* / *bear* is the prettiest.
5 Shelly is *the best* / *the worst* singer in the barn.
6 Rocky says his mum's *the angriest* / *the naughtiest* animal in the barn.

2 Talk about the animals. Ask and answer with a friend.

angriest biggest cleverest naughtiest oldest prettiest worst singer

Who is the worst singer?

Shelly.

1 Read and draw lines.

Three children are looking at the pandas at the zoo. Paul's the oldest and tallest. His sister Vicky's the youngest and shortest. Their sister Sally's got the longest hair. It's blonde and straight. Sally thinks that the smallest panda is the prettiest of the four. Its name is Chu Lin. Vicky thinks Bao Bao is the happiest, but he's also the dirtiest. The fattest panda is Yang Yang, but he isn't the biggest. Gu Gu is the biggest and the oldest. He's 20 years old.

2 Read and write.

1 My dad's the tallest (tall) in our family.
2 The ________ (big) animal in the world is the blue whale.
3 Lily's the ________ (good) singer in the class.
4 The dolphin is one of the ________ (clever) animals in the world.
5 My uncle Peter's the ________ (thin) grown-up in my family.
6 Daisy's got the ________ (curly) hair in the class.
7 My cousin Jim thinks that Monday is the ________ (bad) day of the week.
8 My aunt's the ________ (funny) person in our family.

1 Write the words.

1. evom move
2. pjmu
3. blicm
4. lafl
5. iedh
6. esol
7. kwal
8. nur
9. ylf

2 Read and tick ✓ or cross ✗.

1 
✓
The lion's running.

2 
The panda's falling.

3 
The dolphin's jumping.

4 
The bear's climbing a tree.

5 
The bat's flying.

6 
The rabbit's hiding behind a rock.

1 Look at picture A. Read and write *yes* or *no*.

1 The bat's eating fruit below the fruit tree. no

2 There's a brown bear near a rock. ______

3 The grey bear's behind the brown bear. ______

4 The bat's opposite the monkey. ______

5 The snake is in the tree. ______

6 The parrot is above the tree. ______

A

B

2 Write about the differences. Use these words.

above below near opposite

1 In picture A the monkey is above the bat, but in picture B the monkey is below the bat.

2 ______

3 ______

4 ______

5 ______

6 ______

1 Give the animals the correct food.

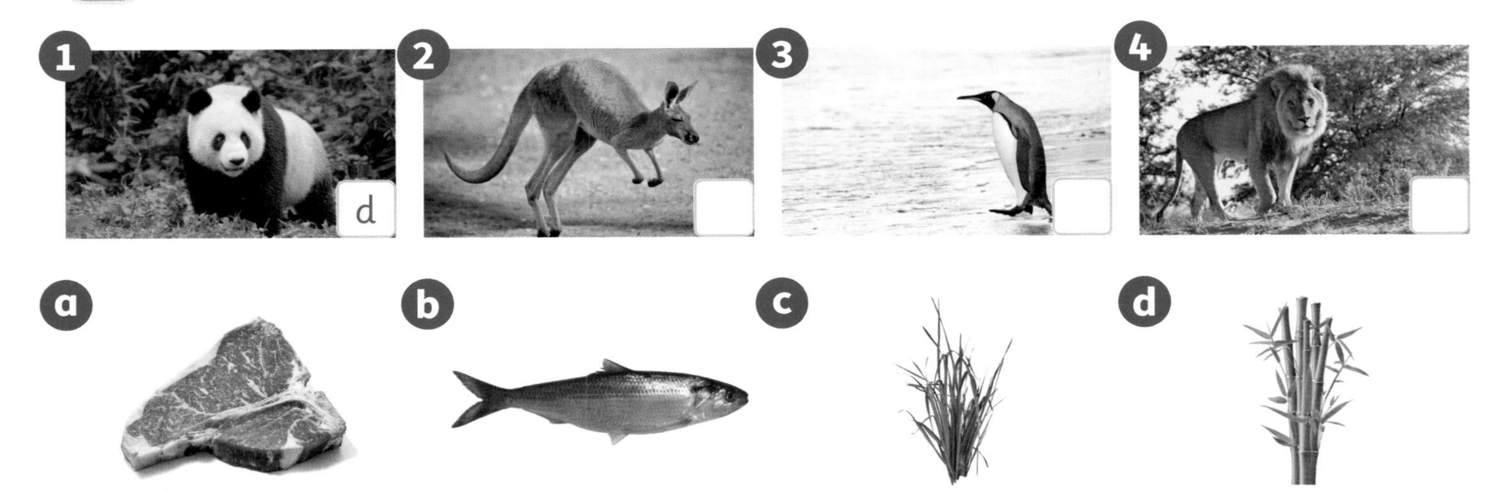

2 Read and match.

1 These animals only eat plants.
2 These animals only eat meat.
3 These animals eat meat and plants.

a Omnivores
b Herbivores
c Carnivores

3 Look at the pictures. Complete the sentences.

1 This is a bear. It eats meat and plants. It is an omnivore.

2 This is ____________.
It eats ____________.
It is ____________.

3 ____________
____________.

4 ____________
____________.

4 Read and guess the animal. Draw.

It lives in Africa.

It is a herbivore.

It eats grass and leaves.

It is big and grey.

It has got four legs, big ears and a long trunk.

It can swim and it can run very fast.

What is it?

It is ______________________ .

5 Write about your favourite wild animal. Draw.

Name: ______________________ Group: ______________________

Colour: ______________________ Lives: ______________________

Characteristics: It has got ______________________ .

It is ______________________ .

It can ______________________ but it cannot ______________________ .

Food: ______________________

1 Put the pictures in order. Then tell the story.

a

b

c

d

e

f

2 Choose a picture from Activity 1. Write a sentence. Read it to a friend. Can they guess which picture it is?

It's a sunny day. A kangaroo is near the river. She is playing with her joey.

---

3 Look at the pictures. Talk about what is happening.

1

2

3

The little boy can't swim. His dad is helping him.

4 Look at the pictures. Talk about the differences.

A

In picture A the kangaroo has got a baby. In picture B it hasn't got a baby.

B

5 Ask and answer.

Have you got a pet?

Yes, I've got a cat.

1 Have you got a pet?

2 What do you do with your pet?

3 What's your favourite animal?

4 Tell me about your favourite animal.

1 Read the text and choose the best answer.

Example

Jim: Are you watching a film, Vicky?
Vicky: (A) Yes, I am.
B Yes, I can.
C Yes, I do.

Questions

1 Jim: Is the film about a kangaroo?
Vicky: A I know it is!
B That's right. It's great!
C It likes jumping!

2 Jim: Is the film funny?
Vicky: A Yes, it is.
B Yes, it did.
C Yes, it can.

3 Jim: I'd like to go to the cinema to see a film.
Vicky: A Me too.
B I liked the film.
C You would go.

4 Jim: Which film would you like to see in the cinema?
Vicky: A You can see good films there.
B I saw a good one last week.
C There's one about bears on this week.

5 Jim: Shall we go on Saturday afternoon?
Vicky: A Good idea!
B So shall I!
C OK, you go.

6 Jim: Why don't we ask Clare to come with us?
Vicky: A Let's watch this together!
B OK, let's do that!
C Why doesn't he come?

1 Play the game.

The bats are sleeping.

INSTRUCTIONS

1 Roll the dice and move your counter.

2 Say what the animals are doing.

6 Our weather

My unit goals

Practise

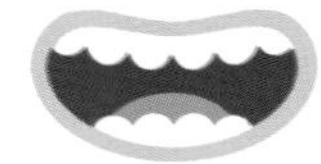

Say and write

new words in English

Learn to say

in English

My mission diary

	Hooray!	OK	Try again

My favourite stage: ______________

Go to page 120 and add to your word stack!

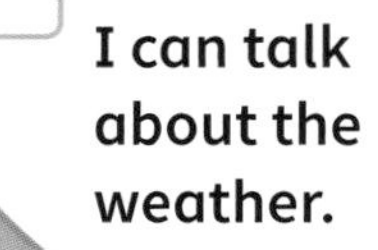

I can talk about the weather.

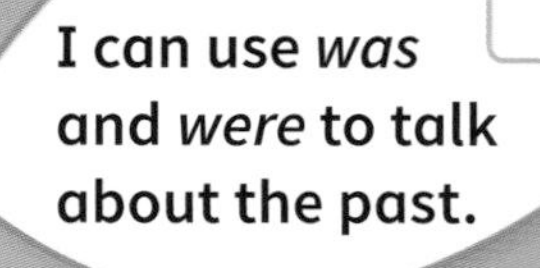

I can use *was* and *were* to talk about the past.

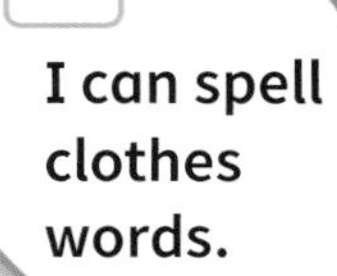

I can spell clothes words.

I can listen for names, numbers and other information.

1 Write the words, then match.

clouds rainbow ~~raining~~ snowing sunny windy

1. We can't go for a walk in the countryside because the weather's terrible. It's raining.
2. It's cold and snows a lot in the mountains. It's ________ today.
3. We can fly our kites at the beach today. It's ________ and it isn't raining. Great!
4. Look Mum, there's a ________ over the roof of that house.
5. Can we go for a swim in the lake Dad? It's hot and ________ .
6. Let's go for a long walk in the forest. It isn't hot; there are a lot of ________ .

Sounds and spelling

2 4.25 Listen and point. Then listen again and say.

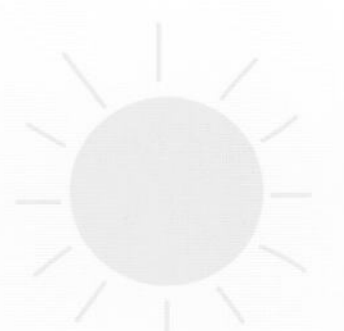

3 4.26 Listen and colour the letters that make the /iː/ sound.

tree bee
three

windy sunny
cloudy

1 Listen, read and correct. 2.34

1. Oh, my hair! It was sunny yesterday and it wasn't ~~hot~~. cold
2. Today, I don't know, but yesterday they were in the forest. ______
3. They were on holiday in the rain. ______
4. I was with my younger cousin and we were out in the fields. ______
5. We were in the snow, but we weren't cold. We were sad. ______
6. Look! It's cloudy and there's a rainbow! ______

2 Ask and answer the questions.

1. Where were Grandma and Grandpa yesterday?
2. What was the weather like?
3. Where were Gracie and her cousin in her story?
4. What was the weather like?
5. Were they happy?

Where were Grandma and Grandpa yesterday?

In the mountains.

1 Read and circle the correct words.

1 It *wasn't* / *weren't* cloudy yesterday. It was windy.
2 Where *was* / *were* they at nine o'clock this morning?
3 I *was* / *were* in the forest with my grandparents last Sunday.
4 Where *was* / *were* she last Wednesday?
5 Why *was* / *were* your socks in the dining room?
6 You *wasn't* / *weren't* at school last Thursday.
7 He *was* / *were* in the bathroom at seven o'clock.
8 The children *wasn't* / *weren't* hot because the window *was* / *were* open.

2 Read and write the words. Answer the questions.

~~was~~ was wasn't were were weren't

Last weekend was brilliant. On Saturday, I 1 was at the beach with my family. We were there all day. It was windy, but it 2 ________ cold. Dad was very happy because the weather was good for flying our new kite. We were on the sand, but we 3 ________ near the sea and the kite was above our heads. It was very funny, because two silly birds 4 ________ above our heads, too. One big one 5 ________ below the kite and another smaller one was above it. They 6 ________ happy, playing with the kite.

1 Where were they on Saturday? They were at the beach.
2 What was the weather like? ________________
3 Why was Dad very happy? ________________
4 Why was it funny? ________________
5 Where were the birds? ________________

1 Put the words in groups.

balcony basement bat bear ~~boots~~ cloud coat
floor parrot rabbit rain roof scarf shorts snow
stairs sunny sweater whale wind

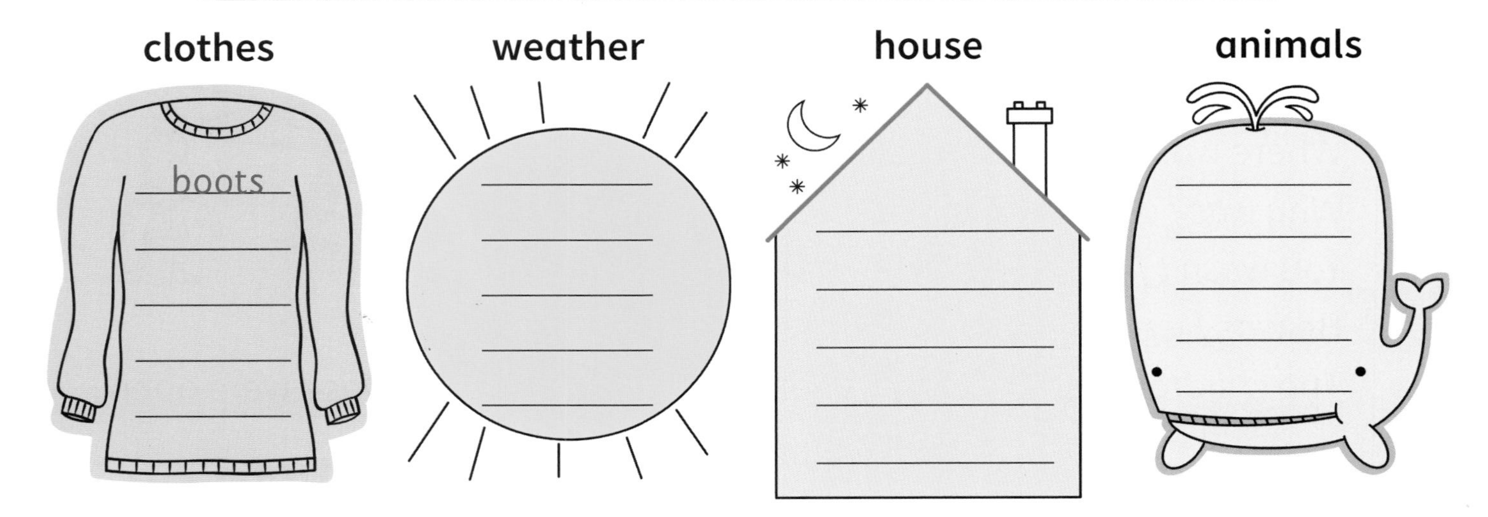

2 Write the words. Find the secret word.

1 It's very cold today. He's wearing his long green scarf.

2 Sorry Sally, you can't ________ your pop-star costume to school.

3 ________ ________ your boots in the house! They're dirty!

4 You need a hat, scarf and ________ because it's cold outside.

5 I ________ ________ my socks before my shoes.

6 She wants to wear her pirate ________ to the party.

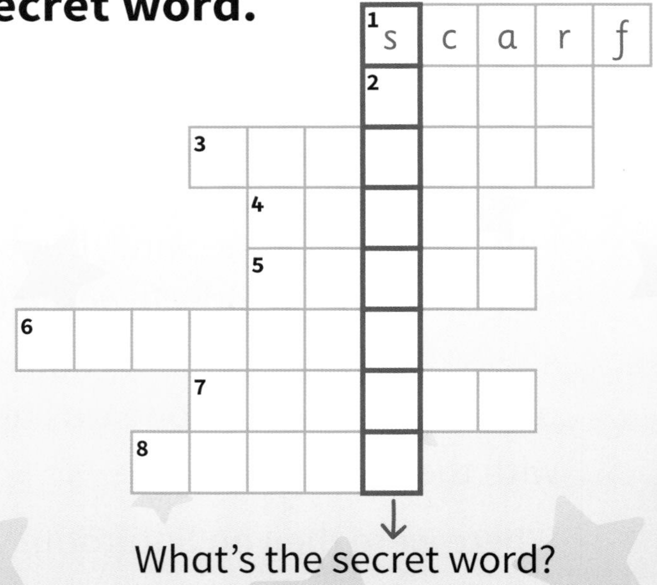

What's the secret word?

____

7 When it's hot we wear a T-shirt and ________.

8 They must put on their ________ to play in the rain.

1 Write the words in the correct order.

1 TV last night / a great / film on / There was / .

There was a great film on TV last night.

2 any leaves / Were / on the trees / there / ?

3 a rainbow above / was / the field / There / .

4 wasn't / the farm / There / a lake opposite / .

5 at the party, but / There were / only one pirate / two clowns / .

2 Read the text and choose the best answer.

1 Where were you yesterday?
- a Yes, that's right.
- b It was nine o'clock.
- (c) I was at home.

2 What was on television?
- a It was windy.
- b A film about animals.
- c My uncle wasn't at home.

3 Were there any bears in the film?
- a No, it wasn't.
- b Yes, there was.
- c Yes, there were.

4 What kind of bears were they?
- a Pandas are black and white.
- b They were big brown bears.
- c My cousin's got a teddy bear.

1 Read and match.

a

b

c
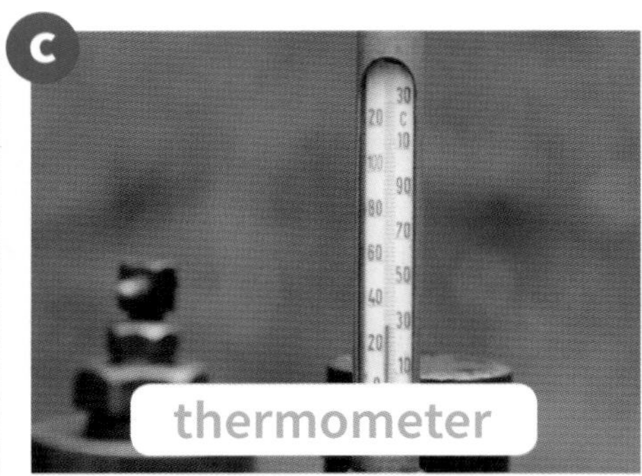

1 This instrument measures how hot or how cold it is. ☐
2 This instrument measures how much rain falls. ☐
3 This instrument shows us the direction of the wind. ☐

2 Make a weather vane.

- card ☐
- a straw ☐
- a pin ☐
- a pencil with a rubber on the end ☐
- scissors ☐
- coloured pencils or pens ☐

1 Draw the head and tail of the weather vane. Decorate them and cut them out.

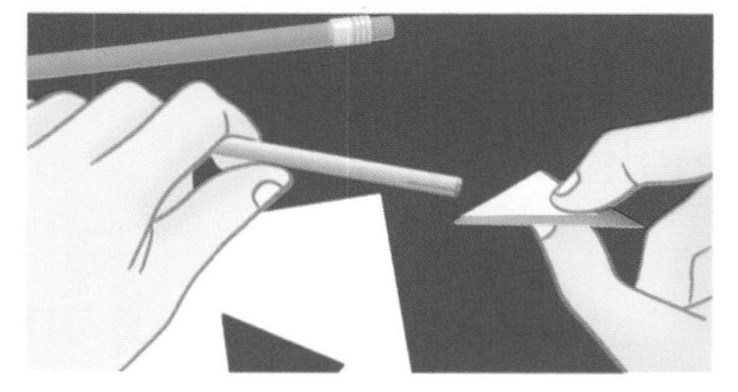

2 Cut both ends of the straw and put the head in one end and the tail in the other.

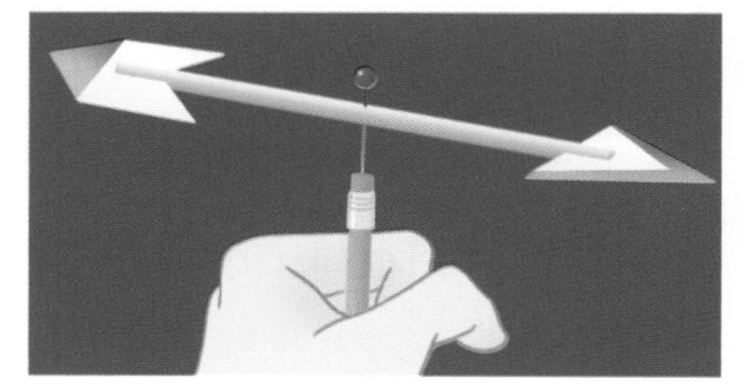

3 Push the pin through the straw and into the rubber of the pencil.

4 Go outside and find the direction of the wind. Have fun!

3 Draw a weather map. Then write.

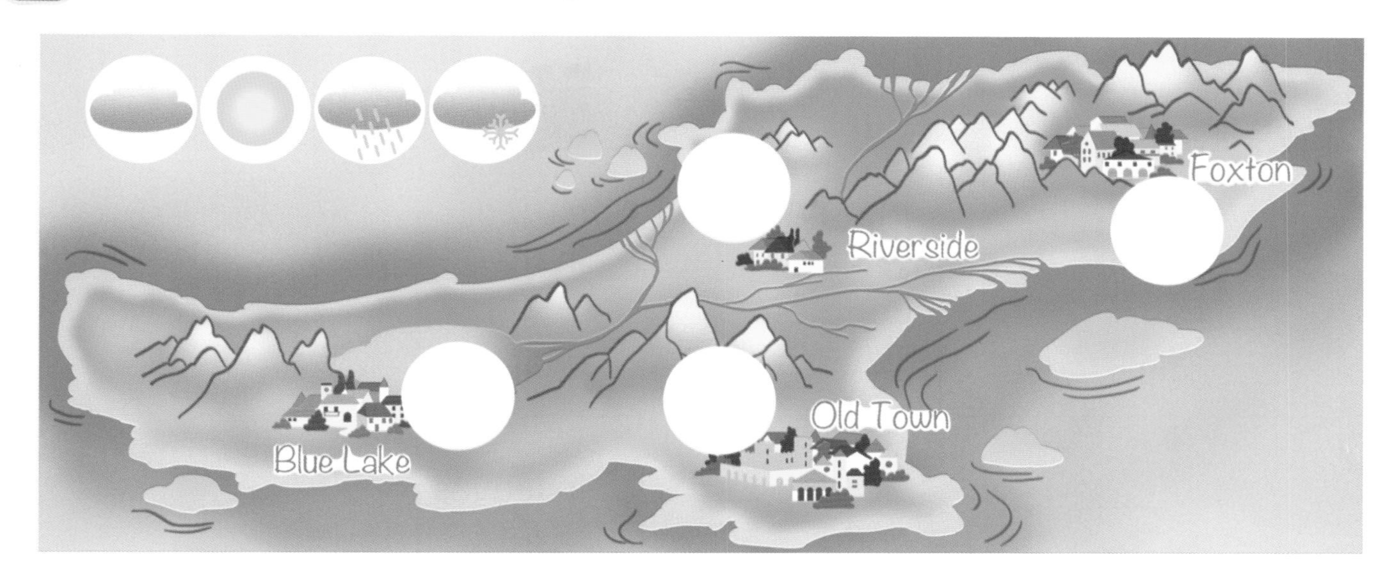

1 It is ______________ in Old Town.

2 It is ______________ in Blue Lake.

3 ______________________________

4 ______________________________

4 Ask and answer questions about your map with a friend.

What's the weather like in Foxton on your island?

It's sunny. What's the weather like in Foxton on your island?

It's raining.

5 Record the weather. Draw the symbols. Then talk with a friend.

Monday	Tuesday	Wednesday	Thursday	Friday

Was it sunny on Monday?

Yes, it was!

1 Complete the table with information from the poem. Write and draw.

Type of weather	Things to do	Type of clothes
1 rain	Imagine you are at sea ________ in the puddles. ________ a lot.	
2 ________	________ in leaves and ________ them around.	
3 ________	________ things in the clouds.	
4 ________	Slide on ________. Make a ________.	

2 What clothes do you wear when it's warm and sunny?

____

3 What can you do when it's sunny? Complete the poem.

The sun is shining all around,
It shines on you and me.
I'm ________.
I'm ________ too!
I'm having fun in the sun.
How about you?

Read the text. Choose the right words and write them on the lines.

Clouds

On planet Earth there 1 ___are___ lots of different types of clouds in the sky.

Some clouds are white, fat and fluffy. They are big and they are high in the sky. Other types of clouds are grey or thin. Sometimes, they are so low we think we can touch them. 2 ________ clouds contain water. The water falls as rain, but 3 ________ it is very cold, the water in the clouds freezes and falls down as 4 ________ .

Watching clouds is lots of fun. 5 ________ we can see dragons or turtles or other shapes. They also tell us what type of weather is 6 ________ . For example, scientists say that green clouds mean that a tornado is coming.

1	is	are	am
2	All	Any	Every
3	what	why	when
4	snow	wind	rain
5	Never	Always	Sometimes
6	come	comes	coming

1 Listen and write. There is one example.

4.27

Go to my grandparents' house

Go at: 12 o'clock

1 Road number: G ______

2 Video call name: Kitty ______

3 In the green bag: ______

4 Play with: ______

5 In the afternoon: Fix ______

2 Listen and draw lines. There is one example.

4.28

Ben Kim Ann Matt

Julia Paul Hugo

1 Play the game.

It was hot and sunny.

INSTRUCTIONS

1 Roll the dice.

2 Move your counter.

3 Pictures: Say what you see.

4 Sentences: Read, find and move to that square.

Review • • • Units 4–6

1 4.29 Listen and circle.

Name	Weather		Where		Clothes	
1 Sally	a	b	a	b	a	b
2 Jane	a	b	a	b	a	b
3 Tony	a	b	a	b	a	b
4 Fred	a	b	a	b	a	b

2 Compare two animals. Use the words from the box.

climb fly jump run swim walk

clever fast fat pretty short slow tall thin

Bat and panda.

A bat can fly, but a panda can't.

A panda is fatter than a bat.

3 Read and draw.

Look at my animal picture. The whale is the biggest animal. It's in the middle of the picture. There's a dolphin above the whale. It's not as big as the whale, but it's bigger than the penguin. The penguin is below the whale. The smallest animal in my picture is near the penguin. It's a bat. There is a rabbit next to the bat.

4 Write about your family. Use words from the boxes.

aunt brother cousin dad grandma grandpa mum sister uncle

clever curly funny long old short straight tall young

1 My grandma's hair is the curliest.

2 ______________________________

3 ______________________________

4 ______________________________

5 ______________________________

6 ______________________________

Let's cook!

My unit goals

Practise	Say and write	Learn to say
 	 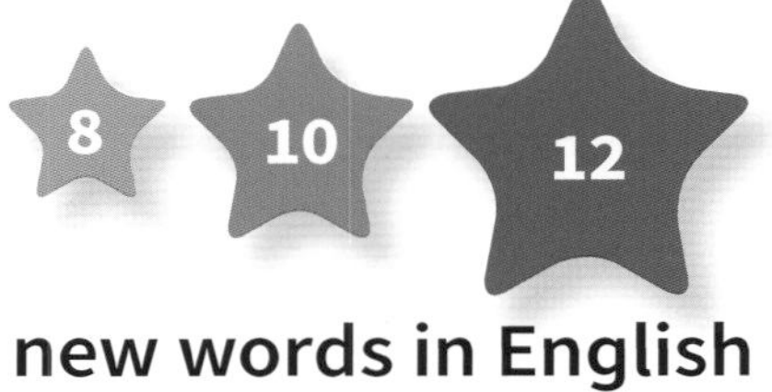 new words in English	in English

(Stars: 8, 10, 12)

My mission diary

	Hooray!	OK	Try again

My favourite stage: ______________

Go to page 120 and add to your word stack!

- [ ] I can name types of food.
- [ ] I can talk and write about cooking.
- [ ] I can talk about things that happened in the past.
- [ ] I can say which picture is different and why.

1 Write the words.

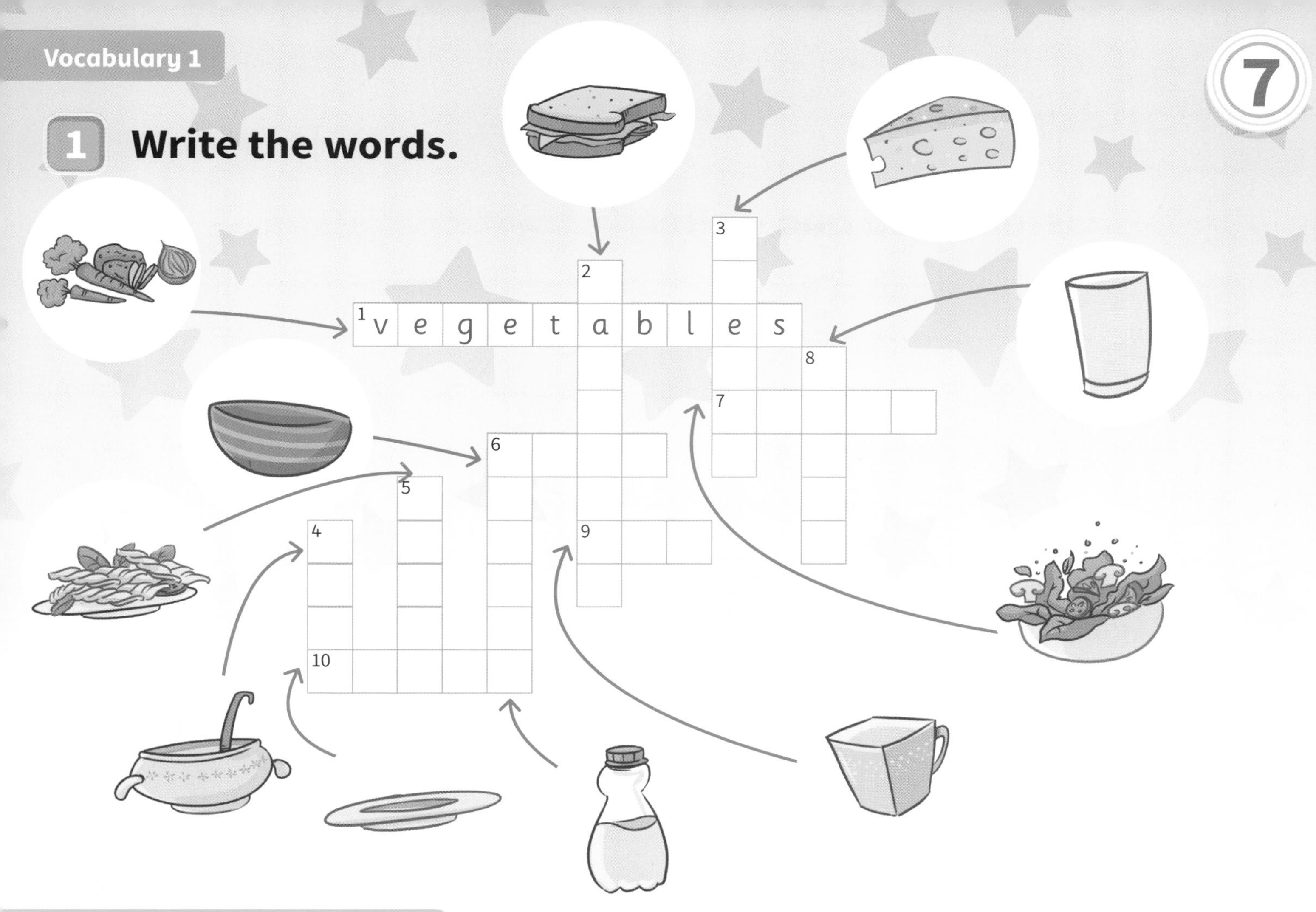

Sounds and spelling

2 4.30 Listen and repeat. Match the words with the pictures.

~~armchair~~ cheese chicken chocolate

3 4.31 Listen and say the tongue twister.

Richie likes eating **ch**icken, **ch**eese and **ch**ocolate in his arm**ch**air!

The Friendly Farm

1 Listen, read and write. 3.05

1 Did they bring the food home?

2 They ate it all at school: soup, sandwiches, pasta, ________ .

3 Yes, I saw them in the ________ yesterday, but I didn't see the food.

4 Did they go ________ ?

5 They got vegetables for ________ .

6 What did you ________ in the soup, Gracie?

2 Ask and answer questions. Use the words from the box.

drink eat have make

Did they eat the food at home?

No, they didn't.

1 Write the sentences in the negative.

1 The children had lunch in the kitchen.

The children didn't have lunch at school.

2 Fred went to the shop to buy some vegetables.

Fred ______________ to the shop to buy a sandwich.

3 Charlie and Sally had a big cheese sandwich at one o'clock.

Charlie and Sally ______________ soup at one o'clock.

4 Jane drank orange juice with her breakfast.

Jane ______________ water with her breakfast.

5 Peter made pasta for dinner.

Peter ______________ pasta for lunch.

2 Read the code and write the text.

	A	B	C	D	E	F
1	last	her	Daisy	potatoes	she	to
2	went	carrot	shops	for	fantastic	carrots
3	was	Saturday	the	were	made	very
4	and	soup	parents	got	lunch	happy

A1 – B3 – C1 – E3 – E4 – D2 – B1 – C4. E1 – A2 – F1 – C3 – C2 – A4 – D4 – F2 – A4 – D1. E1 – E3 – B2 – B4. B1 – C4 – D3 – F3 – F4. C3 – B4 – A3 – E2.

Last Saturday Daisy ______________________________

____

____

____

1 Circle the odd one out. Say why.

A cup is something you use.

1	funny	happy	cup	fantastic
2	wash	soup	pasta	salad
3	kick	drop	hit	sandwich
4	cut	sad	bad	terrible
5	cook	carry	cut	glass
6	aunt	parent	carry	son
7	bottle	drop	cup	bowl
8	cook	boil	plate	fry

2 4.32 Listen and colour.

1 Write the verbs in the past.

~~boil~~ ~~bounce~~ ~~carry~~ ~~clap~~ cook copy cry drop fry hop invite laugh like skate skip smile start stop try wash

+ed	~~y~~+ied	+d	consonant +ed
boiled	carried	bounced	clapped
________	________	________	________
________	________	________	________
________	________	________	________
________	________	________	________

2 Complete the sentences.

1 The children washed their hands before dinner.

2 Last week I ________ my friends to my birthday party.

3 Sally ________ at the camera and her dad got a good photo.

4 The film was very funny. We all ________ a lot.

5 I helped my grandma with the shopping. I ________ the bags.

6 Peter's mum wasn't very happy because he ________ one of her favourite plates.

7 The book was very sad. I ________ at the end.

8 The rain ________ at four o'clock in the afternoon, and the children went outside to play.

1 Look and write the words.

~~flower~~ fruit leaf seeds

1 flower

2 ______

3 ______

4 ______

2 Which part of the plant do we eat?

flowers fruit ~~leaves~~ seeds

1 leaves

2 ______

3 ______

4 ______

3 Colour the food from plants in green and the food from animals in red.

4 Read and match.

1	We use aloe vera	a	they give us oxygen.
2	We use trees	b	to make sun cream.
3	We use cotton plants	c	are medicines.
4	When plants make their food	d	to make clothes.
5	Many plants	e	to make paper.

1 Look and read. Write *yes* or *no*. Explain your answers.

1 Sonny cooks in Uncle Raymond's café.

no He washes plates, bowls, cups and glasses.

2 The cooks from the café were all at home.

_____ __________________________

3 Uncle Raymond doesn't think Sonny can cook in the café.

_____ __________________________

4 Selina Redman asks Uncle Raymond to cook in her restaurant.

_____ __________________________

2 Look at the picture. What happens next? Tick ✓ the best answer.

a Sonny doesn't work in Restaurant Redman. ☐

b Sonny goes to work at Restaurant Redman. Selina is very happy. ☐

c Sonny goes to work at Restaurant Redman. Selina isn't very happy. ☐

3 Ask and answer with a friend.

1 Do you like cooking?

2 What is your favourite thing to cook?

3 What is your favourite thing to eat?

Do you like cooking?

Yes, I do.

4 Read and write the words.

My name is Sonny Miller and I am a 1 ___chef___. I work in Restaurant Redman every Saturday and I love it! I make pasta, soup and salad. I work very hard. When Selina Redman asked me to work in her restaurant, I was very 2 ___________. Selina is a brilliant chef. I always go to her restaurant for my 3 ___________. She makes beautiful cakes!

I don't see Selina very often at the restaurant. She is usually in London making her 4 ___________ show. Do you know it? It's called *In My Kitchen*. I watch it every week! I want to have my own TV show one day.

Before I became a chef, I 5 ___________ dishes in my uncle Raymond's cafe. I didn't like doing that. I love 6 ___________, but I don't like washing dirty bowls, cups and glasses!

sad

~~chef~~

washed

bought

birthday

happy

cooking

television

1 4.33 Which picture is different?

1

2

3

4

1 Play the game.

INSTRUCTIONS

1 Roll the dice and move your counter.
2 Say what the people and animals did.

What did he do?

He made a sandwich.

8

Around town

My unit goals
Practise
Say and write
8
10
12
new words in English
Learn to say
in English
My mission diary
Hooray!
OK
Try again
1
2
3
My favourite stage: ____________
Go to page 120 and add to your word stack!
I can write about a trip.
I can name places in a town.
I can talk about things I have to do.
I can listen and choose the correct picture.

1 Read and match.

car park ~~city centre~~ funfair map
ride road ticket train station

1 The middle of the city where the shops are. city centre
2 We go there to go on fantastic rides. ____________
3 We must buy one to catch a bus or train. ____________
4 You go there to catch a train. ____________
5 This is a place for your car near the shops. ____________
6 We go on this at the funfair. ____________
7 Cars drive on this. It's bigger than a street. ____________
8 We can use this to find places in a city. ____________

Sounds and spelling

How do we write that sound?

2 4.34 Can you hear the /əʊ/ sound? Listen and say *yes* or *no*.

3 4.35 Listen and colour the letters that make the /əʊ/ sound.

1 Listen, read and tick ✓ or cross ✗.

3.24

1 Grandpa Friendly bought his hat last weekend. ✗
2 The family drove to the beach and were there for a week. ☐
3 Henrietta and Rocky rode in Grandpa's lorry. They sat next to him. ☐
4 Grandpa Friendly brought Gracie home. ☐
5 Grandpa Friendly gave them nice vegetables to eat. ☐
6 Grandpa Friendly gave Harry his hat. ☐

2 Read and complete the story with the words from the box.

bought chose ~~found~~ gave told took wore

Harry 1 _found_ Grandpa Friendly's hat in the box. Grandpa 2 ________ it last year and he 3 ________ it on holiday at the beach. He 4 ________ a green one because it's his favourite colour. Harry 5 ________ the other animals that Grandpa 6 ________ him the hat, but he didn't. Harry 7 ________ it from the garden.

1 Read and match. Colour.

1 How many photos did Jane take?	4 Which ice cream did Mary choose?	They gave me some skates.	He fed them at eight o'clock.
2 What did your grandparents give you?	5 What time did Jim feed the fish?	It slept in the garden.	She took five.
3 Where did the rabbit sleep?	6 What did Daisy's parents buy her?	She chose chocolate.	They bought her a new sweater.

2 Complete the sentences in the past.

1 Peter drew (draw) a picture for his mother.
2 Lily ______ (find) a scarf on the bus.
3 He ______ (lose) his kite in the park.
4 Fred's dad ______ (buy) five tickets.
5 Sally ______ (wear) her new yellow boots.
6 Paul's mum ______ (drive) him to school.
7 My cousin ______ (hide) behind the bookcase.
8 Charlie's friends ______ (give) him a fantastic book.
9 I ______ (take) lots of photos on holiday.
10 We ______ (go) on the biggest ride at the funfair.

1 Write the words. Find the secret word.

1 square

2

3

4

5

6

7

8

9

10

11

What is the secret word? ____________________

2 Complete the sentences. Use the words in Activity 1.

1 Jane and her mum sat under a tree in the square and fed the birds.

2 Daisy found some great adventure books in the __________ .

3 Sally's uncle bought some vegetables at the __________ .

4 They went to the __________ __________ and bought some new clothes.

5 Vicky's aunt had a baby boy. Vicky went to the __________ to see her new cousin.

6 Charlie and his dad went to a __________ in the city centre. They drank lemonade.

7 Lily and her friends went to the __________ to see a film.

8 The bus came into the __________ __________ at six o'clock.

1 Read the text and complete the sentences.

Vicky went to her grandparents' house at the beach last weekend. On Friday night her grandfather said, 'Let's go to the funfair tomorrow. We have to get up at six o'clock, because we have to catch the number 27 bus.'

'We don't have to take food because there's a café opposite the funfair,' her grandmother told them.

'That's good,' her grandfather said, 'because I don't have to carry big picnic bags on the rides!' Grandma and Vicky both laughed.

1. Vicky's grandfather wanted to take her to the funfair.
2. They had to ______ at six o'clock to catch the bus.
3. They didn't have to take food because there was a ______ opposite the funfair.
4. Her grandfather was happy because he didn't have to carry the picnic bags on the ______.

2 Write the words in the correct order.

1. Peter has to / to school / a train / catch / .
   Peter has to catch a train to school.
2. have to / seven o'clock / Mary doesn't / get up at / .
   ______
3. wear a / Sally / helmet on her bike / has to / .
   ______
4. My parents / do homework / have to / don't / .
   ______
5. for tests / Do you / study / have to / ?
   ______

1 Look and write the words.

litter bin pavement pedestrian crossing
road ~~road signs~~ street lamp traffic lights

1, 2

3

4

1 road signs
2 ____________
3 ____________
4 ____________

5

6

7

5 ____________
6 ____________
7 ____________

2 How can we keep safe in the city? Read and match.

1 Always walk — d
2 Use a pedestrian
3 Wait for the green man at
4 Remember to stop,
5 Hold hands with a grown-up
6 Don't play with

a a ball near traffic.
b the crossing.
c look, listen and think.
d on the pavement.
e crossing to cross the road.
f when crossing the road.

3 Read and complete. Then match.

look pavement pedestrian crossing ~~road~~

1 You mustn't play in the road.
2 You must walk on the ________.
3 You must cross at the ________.
4 You must ________ when you cross.

a

b

c 1

d

4 How safe are you? Circle your answers.

1	I walk on the pavement.	Always	Sometimes	Never
2	I use the pedestrian crossings.	Always	Sometimes	Never
3	I run across the road.	Always	Sometimes	Never
4	I wait for the green man before I cross the road.	Always	Sometimes	Never
5	I hold my parents' hands when we cross the road.	Always	Sometimes	Never
6	I play with a ball on the pavement.	Always	Sometimes	Never

1 Answer the questions.

1 Why did Tom's mum give him a little push?

Because he didn't want to go on the bus.

2 What was the bus driver's name?

____

3 Who was Tom's bus buddy?

____

4 What could the bus do?

____

5 What could Tom see from the bus?

____

6 Who did Tom see at the end of the story?

____

2 What can you learn from the story? Tick ✓ the best answer.

a School buses are great. ☐

b Don't be scared to try new things. ☐

c Bus buddies are very helpful. ☐

3 Read the text and complete the sentences.

'Can we go to the safari park on my birthday, please?' said Tom. As they drove into the park Tom read the sign.

'You must not feed the animals.'

'Why can't we feed the animals?' he asked.

'Because they are wild animals. They're not pets,' his dad said.

1 Tom wanted to go to the safari park on his birthday.

2 The sign said that they must not ________ the animals.

3 Tom's dad said it was because they were ________ animals.

The car in front stopped. The window opened and a little girl's hand dropped a sandwich out of the window.

'Mum, look at the monkey. It wants to eat the sandwich,' said Tom.

Suddenly, there were a lot of monkeys jumping on the car.

That was the day Tom learned that it is very important to read the signs.

4 He saw a little girl drop a ________ out of the window.

5 Lots of monkeys ________ on the car.

6 The little girl got into problems because she ________ read the signs.

1 Listen and tick (✓) the box. There is one example.

Where is Peter going with his mother?

a 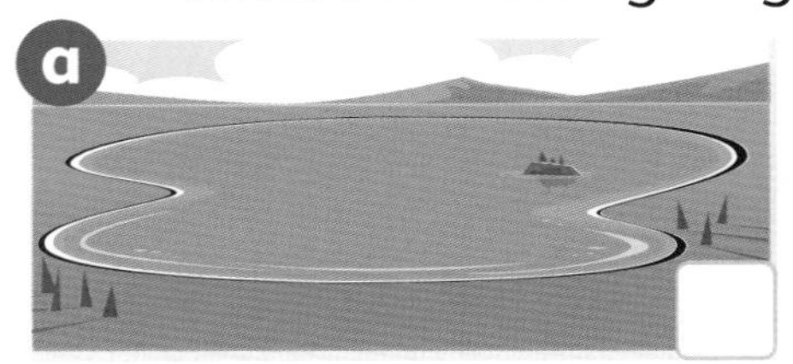

b 

c 

1 Which girl is Mr Ball's granddaughter?

a 

b 

c 

2 Which sweater does Sam want to wear for the party?

a 

b 

c 

3 Where was Zoe on Monday?

a 

b 

c 

4 What is Fred doing now?

a 

b 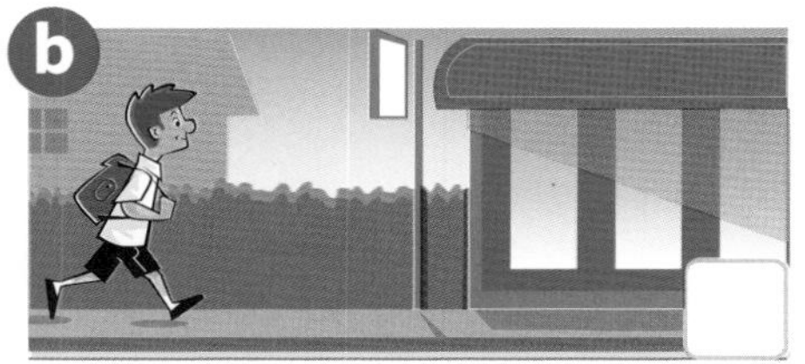

c 

5 Which is the new building in the city?

a 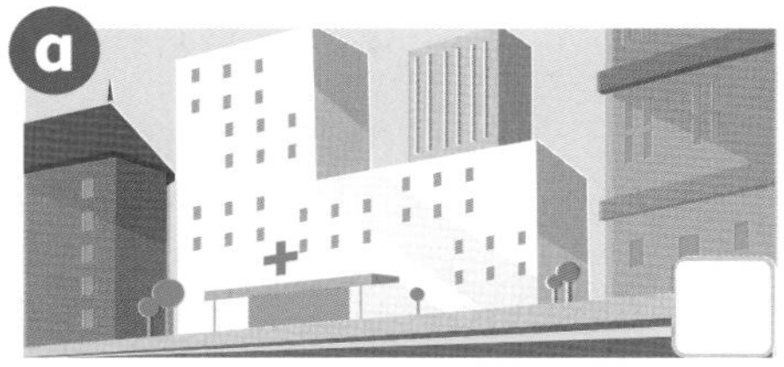

b 

c 

1 Play the game.

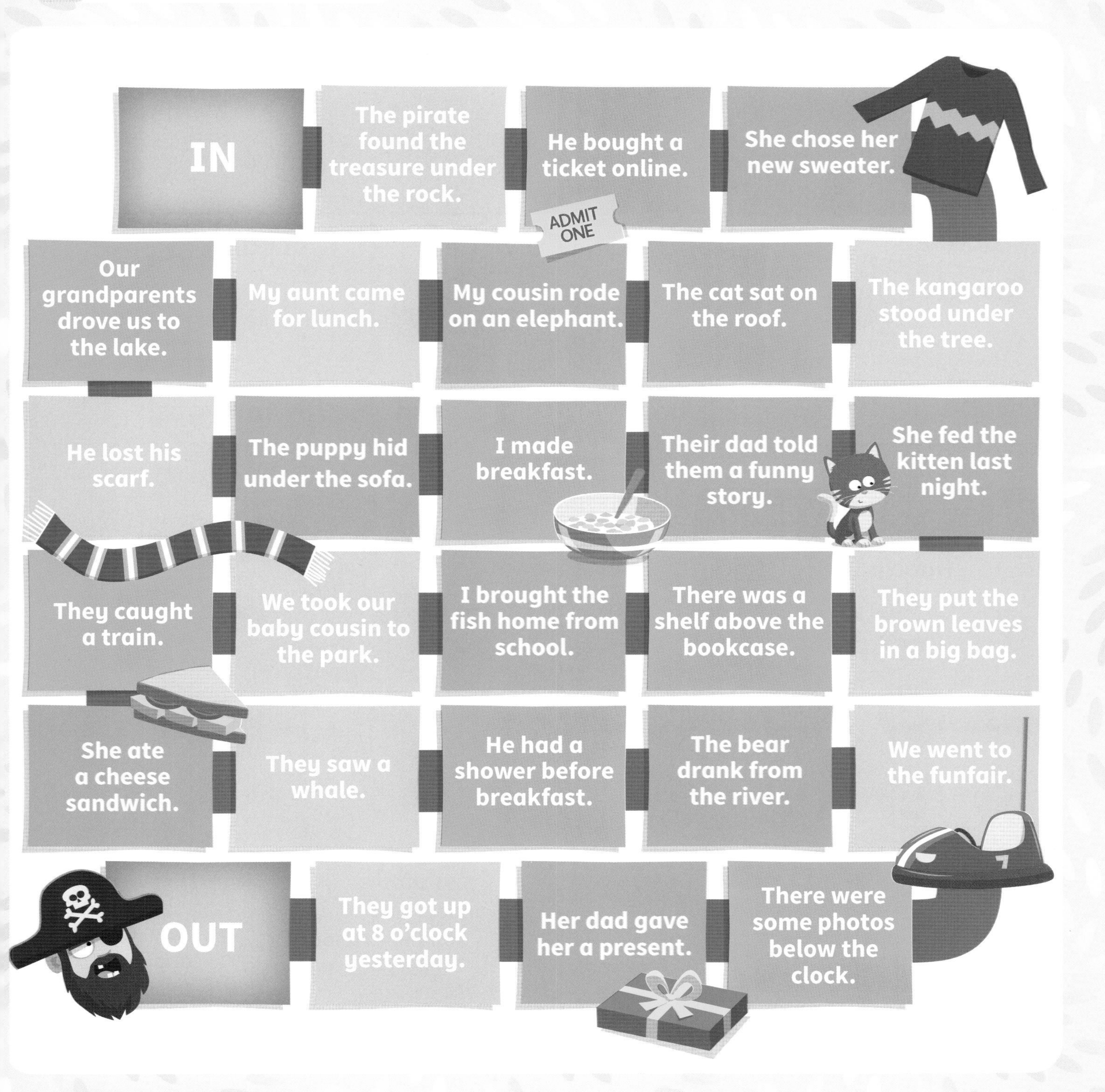

INSTRUCTIONS

1 Roll the dice and move your counter.

2 Make the sentence negative.

The pirate didn't find the treasure under the rock.

9 A big change

My unit goals

Practise

Say and write

8 10 12

new words in English

Learn to say

in English

My mission diary

	Hooray!	OK	Try again

My favourite stage: ______________

Go to page 120 and add to your word stack!

- [ ] I can understand sentences about how people are feeling.
- [ ] I can use *more* and *most* to compare things.
- [ ] I can talk about holidays and adventures.
- [ ] I can read a story and choose the best title.

1 Write the words.

~~afraid~~ boring dangerous difficult easy exciting
frightened hungry thirsty tired surprised

1 I'm afraid of the dark.
2 The exam was really ____________. I got everything right.
3 I love adventure films. They're really ____________.
4 It's ____________ to see in the dark.
5 I'm ____________ of spiders. They make me afraid.
6 The film was so ____________, I fell asleep.
7 Jim slept on the train because he was very ____________.
8 Daisy had to drink a glass of water because she was very ____________.
9 You have to wear a helmet because skateboarding is ____________.
10 Jane gave her mother a secret party. She was very ____________.
11 Mary ate three bananas because she was very ____________.

Sounds and spelling

2 Listen and point to the letters.

3 4.37 Listen again and complete the words.

1 exciting
2 w____________d
3 bor____________
4 pengu____________
5 dolph____________
6 swimm____________

1 Listen and circle the correct words. (3.41)

1. I think your mother's more *tired* / *surprised* than me.
2. The circus is more *boring* / *exciting* than the farm!
3. Jumping and catching are *dangerous* / *easy*.
4. Circus clothes are more *difficult* / *beautiful* than these.
5. He isn't *afraid* / *hungry*.
6. We're in the Friendly Circus. I'm riding Harry. I'm not *frightened* / *surprised*.

2 Read and write the words.

circus dangerous exciting ~~grandparents~~ rode surprised

1. Jim and Jenny's parents told the grandparents that they wanted to work for Diversicus.
2. Grandma was more __________ than Grandpa.
3. Rocky said that a circus was more __________ than a farm and he thought it was a great idea.
4. Gracie was afraid because she thought jumping and catching were more __________ than playing music.
5. The animals wanted to have a __________ in the barn.
6. Shelly sang, Cameron jumped and Rocky __________ on Harry.

1 Write the words in the correct order.

1 skateboarding's / than roller skating / Mary thinks / more exciting / .

Mary thinks skateboarding's more exciting than roller skating.

2 more dangerous / rabbits / are / than / Bears / .

____

3 beautiful / more / than bats / Daisy / lions / thinks that / are / .

____

4 Jim was / At the funfair, / than Jenny / more frightened / .

____

5 than riding / Jack thinks / a bike / climbing's / more difficult / .

____

2 Circle the word that is true for you. Tell your friend.

What do you think?

1	Horse riding's more dangerous than climbing.	yes	no
2	Swimming's more difficult than riding a bike.	yes	no
3	Watching TV's more boring than playing outside.	yes	no
4	Parrots are more beautiful than lions.	yes	no
5	Funfairs are more exciting than skateboarding.	yes	no

I think horse riding is less dangerous than climbing.

1 Find three words in a line from the same group.

1

map	hungry	exciting
sweater	frightened	world tour
dangerous	fall	adventure

2

busy	cinema	email
drive	hospital	market
travel	library	café

3

letter	text	email
costume	cage	world tour
fry	fall	café

4

journey	map	phone
family	travel	circus
exciting	ride	trip

2 Read the text. Choose the right words and write them on the lines.

People enjoy 1 travelling____. They like to fly or drive around the world. Some people look 2 ________ hot weather, sand and beaches; others want to do sport. People use 3 ________, phones or computers to find places to go to and new things to do. They like telling 4 ________ friends and families about their journeys. The 5 ________ way to do this is by text or email with their mobile phones or tablets. Letters are very slow. In many towns there are internet cafés where people can write and send 6 ________ to their friends in other places or countries.

1	travelled	travelling	travel
2	for	at	on
3	trips	maps	stairs
4	his	hers	their
5	easiest	easy	easier
6	falls	emails	boils

1 Look and read. Write *yes* or *no*.

Jim loves climbing in the mountains. He thinks it's the most exciting sport. Jim always climbs with his mum. His dad doesn't climb with them because he thinks it is one of the most dangerous hobbies.

Last year Jim wanted to climb one of the most difficult mountains near their town, but his mum thought it wasn't the best idea. Jim fell and was very frightened but his mum helped him to get down to the ground. His dad drove them home. They were tired, cold and hungry. Jim learnt a lot that day and now he chooses easier mountains to climb.

1. Jim loves climbing in the mountains. ___yes___
2. He thinks it's the most boring sport. ________
3. Jim's dad thinks it's one of the most dangerous hobbies. ________
4. Last year Jim wanted to climb one of the easiest mountains. ________
5. His mum thought it was the best idea. ________
6. Jim dropped his bottle of water and was very thirsty. ________
7. His father drove them home. ________
8. Now Jim chooses easier mountains to climb. ________

2 4.38 Listen and write.

School trip

1. Went to mountains by: ___train___
2. Name of mountains: ________ Mountains
3. Number of children: ________
4. Which animal: ________
5. What food: chicken ________
6. What drink: ________ juice

1 Colour the continents.

Africa – green
Europe – yellow
Asia – orange
North America – blue
South America – red
Australia – purple
Antarctica – pink

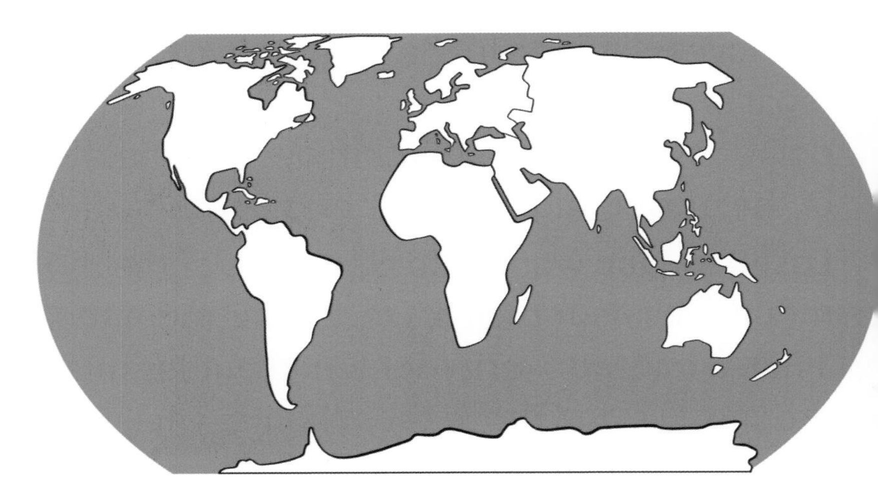

2 Look and match. Write the continent.

Great Barrier Reef   Machu Picchu   Stonehenge   Taj Mahal   ~~Victoria Falls~~

1

Victoria Falls   Africa

2

_______ _______

3

_______ _______

4

_______ _______

5

_______ _______

3 Are these beautiful places natural or manmade?

1 

River Amazon

natural

2 

Stonehenge

______

3 

The Acropolis

______

4 

Mount Everest

______

5 

Niagara Falls

______

6 

The Great Wall of China

______

4 Write sentences.

1 

The Grand Canyon

This is ______.

It is in ______.

2 

The Great Pyramid

This is ______.

It is in ______.

1 Read and correct.

1 The picnic was at Richard's house.

The picnic was in the wood.

2 Richard's mother hid the clues.

3 All of the clues were in the trees.

4 There was a tree like a tiger in the wood.

5 The last clue was 90 steps from the picnic.

2 Find words that rhyme.

around behind Ben ~~do~~ eat everyone giraffe good know news shiver tree

1	two	do	7	laugh	
2	wood		8	see	
3	fun		9	clues	
4	ground		10	go	
5	find		11	river	
6	ten		12	treat	

3 Work in small groups. Have a treasure hunt in your classroom. Write five clues to the secret treasure. Follow another group's clues.

Listen and tick ✓ the box.

1 What is the book about?

a 

b 

c 

2 Whose party is it?

a 

b 

c 

3 Where's the picnic?

a 

b 

c 

4 Which competition is Ana in?

a 

b 

c 

1 Read the story. Choose a word from the box. Write the correct word next to numbers 1–5. There is one example.

Last week Lily and her mum went to see Lily's Uncle Pat. He lives on an *island* . On Saturday morning Pat took Mum and Lily to see all the animals, fruit and (1) ______________ in that place. Lily took lots of photographs. 'Everything is very different here,' said Lily. 'I want to tell Dad about this place.' 'Why don't you send him an email, with some (2) ______________ too?' said Mum. In the evening, Lily wrote to Dad, but she couldn't put the pictures from her camera into the computer. 'Why don't you look for some on the internet?' said Mum. Lily looked at lots of different animals. 'Is this a picture of the (3) ______________ we saw?' she asked. 'I think it was bigger than that and it had a longer (4) ______________,' said Mum. 'But ask Pat – he can help you.' 'Good idea,' said Lily, and she went (5) ______________ to her uncle.

Example

lizard	pictures	tail	island	downstairs
vegetables	hungry	computer	pirate	

2 Now choose the best name for the story. Tick ✓ one box.

Lily's Uncle Pat ☐ Lily's drawings ☐ Lily's beach ☐

1 Play the game.

Where did you go?

I went to the market.

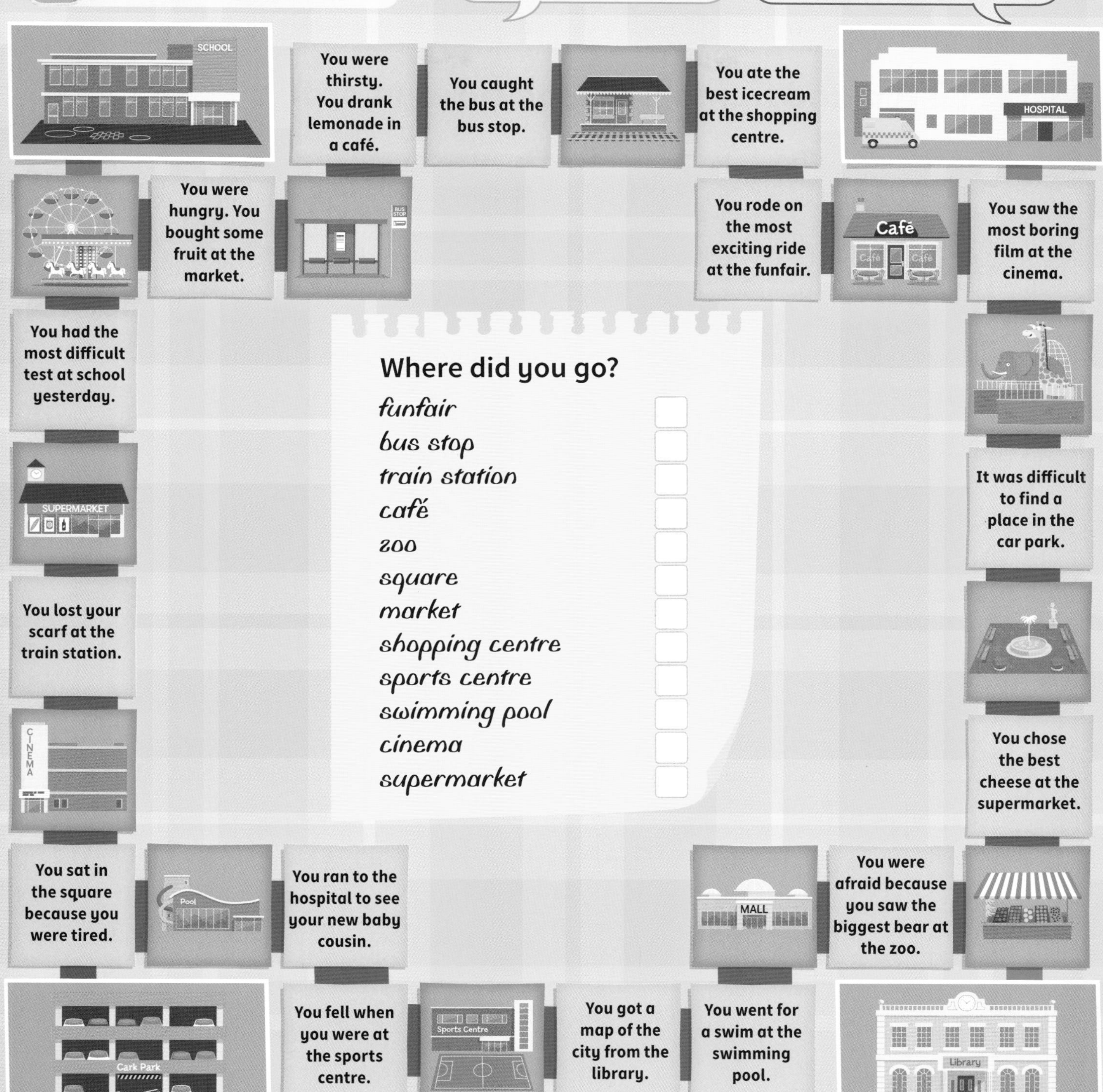

INSTRUCTIONS

1 Choose a place to start.

2 Tick four places on your list.

3 Roll the dice and move your counter.

4 Visit the places on your list.

Review ••• Units 7–9

1 Listen and number the pictures in order. (4.40)

a 

b 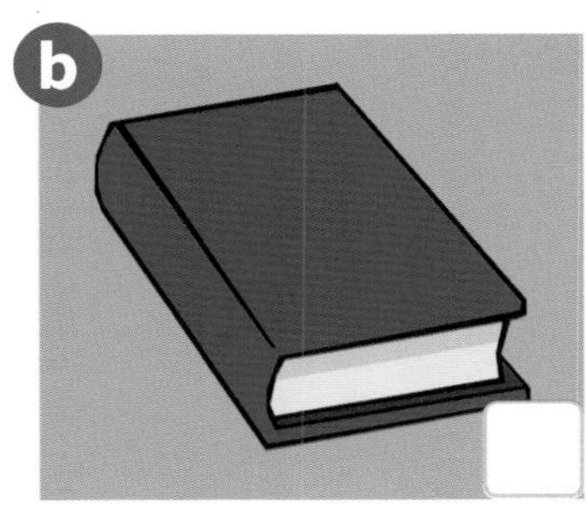

c 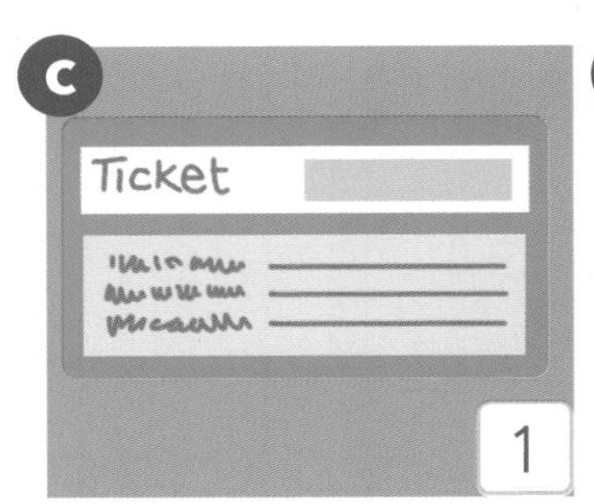

d 

e 

f 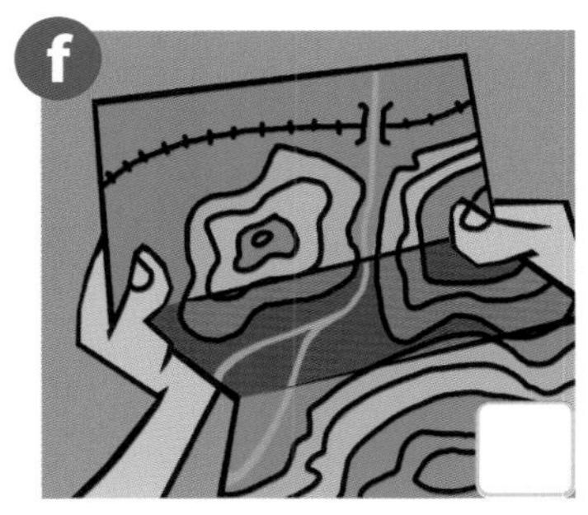

g 

h 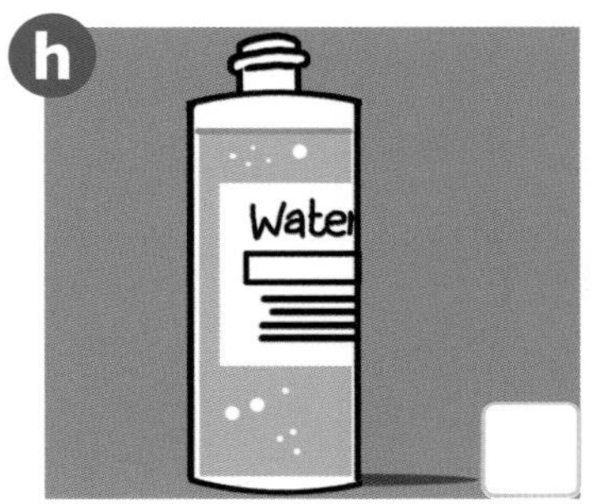

2 Look at the code. Write the words.

a	b	c	d	e	f	g	h	i	j	k	l	m
20	25	27	30	35	39	40	45	47	50	51	55	63
n	**o**	**p**	**q**	**r**	**s**	**t**	**u**	**v**	**w**	**x**	**y**	**z**
65	66	69	71	73	74	81	84	85	87	93	98	99

(73 47 30 35) 74 81 20 81 47 66 65 35 63 20 47 55 63 20 69
81 73 47 69 81 35 93 81 81 73 20 85 35 55 87 66 73 55 30

1 ride 2 ______ 3 ______ 4 ______
5 ______ 6 ______ 7 ______ 8 ______

3 Use the code. Dictate a word to your friend.

63 20 30 35

Is it 'made'?

4 Talk about Sally and Jack. Ask and answer with a friend.

	Make lunch?	Wash vegetables?	Fry onions?	Cook pasta?	Cut bread?	Cut cheese?
Sally	✓	✓	✓	✗	✓	✗
Jack	✓	✗	✗	✓	✓	✓

Did Sally make lunch?

Yes, she did.

5 Draw faces and write why.

frightened ~~hungry~~ surprised thirsty tired

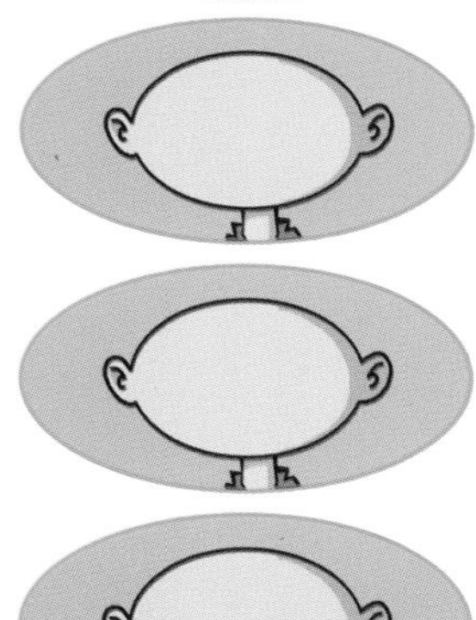

She's hungry because she dropped her soup!

1 Write your favourite new words.